Joomla! Development
A Beginner's Guide

written by Hagen Graf,
Andrea Tarr, Alex Andrea, OpenTranslators, Radek Suski

cocoate

Joomla!
Development
A Beginner's Guide

Introduction 8

The Problem.8

The Solution.8

Coding? 9

What Can You Learn From This Book?.9

How to Start?.9

Prepare Your Workstation 11

Source Code Editors.11

Integrated Development Environments (IDE) 12

What Are Professional Developers Using?.12

Lamp Software Bundle.13

Other Tools.14

What Do I Need?.14

Write Your Own Component 16

Model-View-Controller Architecture.16

Is It Necessary to Build A Component From Scratch? 17

How to Start?.17

The Cocoate Real Estate Component.18

Step 1 - The Basics 19

Frontend and Backend.19

Files and Installation.20

Discover Extension.20

Install Extension.21

The Code.21

Step 2 - Database, Backend, Languages 26

Cocoate Real Estate (CRE) Version 0.0.2 Screenshots.26

CRE Version 0.0.2 Files 29

Database Table cocoaterealestate_objects.30

Models, Tables, Fields, Language Files 32

Controllers 39

Views in Frontend and Backend.40

The Cool Stuff 47

What Is Missing in Our Component?.47

The Future of Cocoate Real Estate.48

The Deal.48

mod_contact_list.xml.51

mod_contact_list.php.54

helper.php.55

tmpl/default.php.57

language/en-GB/en-GB_mod_contact_list.ini.57

language/en-GB/en-GB_mod_contact_list.sys.ini.58

index.html.58

Packaging the Module for Installation.58

Write Your Own Plugin 60

Example.61

Write Your Own Template Overrides 64

More Information on Overrides.68

Write Your Own Layout Alternative 69

Example for Module Alternative Layouts.70

Alternative Menu Items.71

Read More:.71

Write Your Own App Using Joomla! Platform.......................72

History.72

Using the Joomla Platform.73

A Web App.77

Multiple Web Apps 79

More Resources.79

Common Mistakes 81

Radek Suski's List of Common Mistakes 82

YOUR List of Common Mistakes.85

Publish Your Extension to the Joomla! Extension Directory ..86

Publish Your Extension.87

What Is Git? 90

Centralised Repository.90

Commit.91

Merge.91

Versions.91

Distributed Revision Control.91

Decentralised Workflow.91

Dictator and Lieutenants Workflow.92

The Name and the History.92

GitHub.92

Joomla! and GitHub.92

How to Start?.93

More to Read About Git.93

Contribute Code to the Project...95

My Findings.95

Joomla! Leadership.95

Contribute Code In a Technical Way.98

Propose New Features 98

More to Read: 99

Localisation Using OpenTranslators 101

i18n & L10n - why they matter to Joomla extension Developers.102

Transifex 104

OpenTranslators.104

Setting up your project with Transifex & OpenTranslators.106

Volunteer Translators & you.109

Conclusion.110

Running a Business Around Joomla! Extensions 112

The 4 Major Roles of An Extension Business 113

1. Product.113

2. Business Model.113

3. Support.116

4. Promotion.116

5. Hard Work and Discipline Pays Off 117

What Is PHP?...118

Where Is My PHP?.119

Hello World.120

Variables.121

Functions.121

Parameters 122

Control Structures 123

Classes.127

What Is Object-Oriented Programming? 129

Classes, Objects, Instances, Properties and Behaviours.129

Attributes/Properties 130

Instantiation.131

Methods, Behaviours.131

Access Rights.132

How to Use the OOP Paradigm in A Website?.133

Why MooTools? 134

Demos.135

Joomla! and MooTools.135

A Tooltip Example.136

Customised Tooltips with CSS 138

Multiple Customised Tooltips.140

Resources 141

cocoate.com 143

Spend Your Holidays in Southern France 144

Chapter 1

Introduction

Photo: http://www.flickr.com/photos/npobre/2601582256/ (CC BY 2.0)

Using Joomla! is easy. To configure it, you usually use your browser and the Joomla! user interface in front- and backend.

Enhancing Joomla! with additional features is easy, too. You download the desired extension, install it, configure it and use it.

THE PROBLEM

Sometimes you have a request and no idea how to implement it. You searched the Joomla! extension directory but found nothing, no extension that fits your needs.

Let's say you want to start your own real estate business and no extension is on the market that makes you happy because your idea of selling houses is unique!

THE SOLUTION

If there is no predefined solution for your problem you have three possibilities to solve it

1. Think about your problem whether it is honestly that unique. Explore existing real estate solutions and take your time to play around with them. You can learn a lot from existing solutions and maybe you realise that it is possible to use a ready-made solution. That means **no coding**.

2. Use one of the upcoming content construction kits for Joomla! to implement your individual solution. That means **no coding**, too.

3. If you have a budget, think about outsourcing and **pay others for coding**.

4. Or ... start to code! Write your desired extension yourself.

CODING?

When configuring Joomla! via the administrator interface, you already have used different kinds of 'code'.

Visual Code

The visual code is the design of check boxes, options and text fields, different editors, which makes it possible to configure options and add, edit and delete content.

Structural Code

The structural code in Joomla! are words like *templates*, *categories*, *options*, *articles*, *menu items*, *modules*, *styles* and many more. You have to know the meaning of these codes, otherwise you are lost.

'Real Code'

This is what this book is about!

You probably know all these abbreviations like PHP, CSS, JavaScript, HTML, JDOC, XML, and so on. Besides the other meanings mentioned above, the verb 'to code' means to me writing commands into text files, which make sense in a given context. The 'only' challenge you have to face is to learn what all these different commands and contexts are about and how to write them in a way so they work as expected, and are secure, flexible, reliable, fast, and easy to understand.

No one that I know knows all the details of the above-mentioned abbreviations. Some people tend to like Java Script, some PHP, some CSS and some nothing at all.

WHAT CAN YOU LEARN FROM THIS BOOK?

Even if you have never touched a text file with code inside and even if you have no idea at the moment what I am talking about, try to read a few chapters. I don't want to say you'll get enlightened but I think it's just interesting to see the relationships between all these bits and pieces in Joomla!

In the next chapters, I want to cover the main concepts in Joomla! to be able to enhance it with self-made extensions.

HOW TO START?

You need to know many things which have no direct relationship to Joomla!

The Story of mod_coco_bookfeed module

I'll give you a typical example how things happen sometimes.

In the past couple of months people asked me more and more often whether it is possible to place a link to the download of our free books on their website.

They wanted to have the cover of the book in various sizes, the title, the amounts of file downloads and, in the administration interface, a choice of the book to present and so on ...

Saturday, November 12 2011

I started to play around thinking of a solution which offers code to embed but that doesn't work well for the display and the counting of the amount of downloads in the widget, so I decided to create a Joomla! module for that purpose.

Here Is the Story So Far

• I installed a local Joomla! 1.7 on my machine to play around

• I created the structure by copying an existing Joomla! module

• I created a file on our server (cocoate.com) with the necessary data

• I found a possibility to access the server file in the Joomla! module, implemented the features, tested everything and it seemed to work

• I wrote a blog entry and asked for testers (Book Feeds Joomla! Module)[1]

• I got immediately the following feedback:

  • the way I deal with the server file doesn't work on all servers (jwillin)[2]

  • ot2sen[3] enhanced the module with language files and send it to me via email

Wow, that was all in less than 24 hours and it seemed to be possible to work together on that module!

1. For a healthy collaboration I decided to create a project on GitHub (https://github.com/hagengraf/mod_coco_bookfeed)[4]

2. I decided to describe the story of this little module here in the introduction

3. I thought about a further development of the module

In this little example you see a lot of what is necessary and what you need to know when starting with programming in Joomla! You need to know something about Web servers, Editors, local server environment, live server environment, Joomla!, PHP, HTML, XML, Joomla! modules, GIT and, of course, about your possible collaborators.

The following chapters try to cover all or hopefully most of the steps you need to know when you want to start with Joomla! development.

---

[1] http://cocoate.com/node/10189

[2] http://twitter.com/#!/jwillin

[3] http://twitter.com/#!/ot2sen

[4] https://github.com/hagengraf/mod_coco_bookfeed

Chapter 2

Prepare Your Workstation

Photo: http://www.flickr.com/photos/lenore-m/2514975647/ (CC BY 2.0)

In former times, people usually used one workstation to work and all the other devices (if they had one or more) for something different. Today, the situation is changing because of the amount of 'other devices' and the way they are used. Internet access is available in many places and it is often not that easy to distinguish between work and 'the rest'.

You probably have a kind of personal computer and that is your 'workstation'. This doesn't have to be the latest version. Even if you have an older PC, it is easily possible to develop for Joomla!.

Joomla! extensions consist of source code. Source code is text written in a computer programming language. It needs to be written and it needs to be edited. Therefore you need a source code editor. It can be a standalone application or it may be built into an integrated development environment (IDE).

SOURCE CODE EDITORS

Many people start their career as a developer with easy code in simple editors. Each operating system comes with a plain text editor. So often the 'hello world' example is created with

- Windows: Notepad[5]
- OSX: TextEdit[6]
- Linux: VI[7]

You can use these editors for your very first steps. It is also useful to know the basic behaviour and commands of these editors if you have to edit source code on another machine than yours (e.g. your live server). Especially in the case of VI it is important to know how to insert and delete text and how to save the edited file (Basic VI Commands[8]).

After the first steps, you'll notice that it would be nice to have more features like splitting the screen to see more than one file, 'fold' the source code to have a better overview or search in all files of a folder and more unlimited other features.

When you are in that stage, have a look at more advanced editors like

- Windows: Notepad++[9],
- OSX: TextWrangler[10],
- Linux: KDE Advanced Text Editor[11],

INTEGRATED DEVELOPMENT ENVIRONMENTS (IDE)

Joomla! is using the model view controller (MVC) concept as the key concept in developing extensions. Using that concept, you have to write a lot and, therefore, you soon wish to have something which enables you to be more productive. Thus, an IDE like Eclipse[12] or Komodo[13] can be useful.

This is a 45 minutes webinar about using Eclipse[14]

WHAT ARE PROFESSIONAL DEVELOPERS USING?

I asked a question in Facebook[15] and got a lot of answers (*Figure 1*)

---

[5] http://en.wikipedia.org/wiki/Notepad_(software)

[6] http://en.wikipedia.org/wiki/Textedit

[7] http://en.wikipedia.org/wiki/Vi

[8] http://www.cs.colostate.edu/helpdocs/vi.html

[9] http://en.wikipedia.org/wiki/Notepad++

[10] http://en.wikipedia.org/wiki/Notepad++

[11] http://en.wikipedia.org/wiki/Kate_(text_editor)

[12] http://en.wikipedia.org/wiki/Eclipse_(software)

[13] http://www.activestate.com/komodo-ide

[14] http://community.joomla.org/blogs/community/828-webinar-using-eclipse-for-joomla-development.html

[15] http://www.facebook.com/questions/10150247434712168

Figure 1: Facebook Question

A few quotes from Joomla! developers:

> Most Notepad++ and Netbeans (Brian Rønnow, Denmark)

> Switched almost completely to PHPStorm but some smaller things I still do in TextMate. Some older projects are still under Coda control. (Achim Fischer, Germany)

> For dev I use eclipse, for quick edits I'll use Coda. (Chad Windnagle, USA)

> notepad++ and Eclipse (Ronni K. G. Christiansen, Denmark)

> Notepad++ and Netbeans :) (Jeremy Wilken, USA)

> I find Quanta Plus awesomely handy. Mind that I mostly use it for web page editing. Of all the editors I could find in the Canonical repositories I liked Quanta Plus the most. It would take much time to list all that I like about it so I won't do it here. :-) (Alexey Baskinov, Russia)

> For development basically only Eclipse. For quick edits also, Komodo Edit (Radek Suski, Germany)

> It depends on which file / which purpose of editing. Zend Studio and Notepad++ are my choice. (Viet Vu, Vietnam)

LAMP SOFTWARE BUNDLE

LAMP is an acronym for a solution stack of free, open source software, originally coined from the first letters of Linux (operating system), Apache HTTP Server, MySQL and Perl/PHP/Python, principal components to build a viable general purpose web server.

The exact combination of software included in a LAMP package may vary, especially with respect to the web scripting software, as PHP may be replaced or supplemented by Perl and/or

Python. Similar terms exist for essentially the same software suite (AMP) running on other operating systems.

Suitable for beginner's are XAMPP[16], available for Windows, OSX and Linux, WampServer[17] for Windows and MAMP[18] for OSX. They are all easy-to-install Apache Web server distributions containing the latest MySQL Database and PHP script language and they are really very easy to install and to use - just download, extract and start.

OTHER TOOLS

As browsers, you need the usual suspects: Internet Explorer, Chrome, Firefox, Opera, Safari. You need to verify your results in all these web browsers.

All of these browsers offer the possibility to install additional plugins such as Firebug[19] and Webdeveloper[20].

WHAT DO I NEED?

As already mentioned before, start with the editor of your choice and install a Lamp Software Bundle that fits your needs. Install a fresh copy of Joomla! without example data.

• Editor

• Lamp Software Bundle

• The actual Joomla! Version 1.7/2.5

For this book I am using OSX as the operating system, TextWrangler and MAMP. As a browser, I use mainly Firefox with the plugin Firebug.

---

[16] http://www.apachefriends.org/

[17] http://www.wampserver.com/

[18] http://www.mamp.info/

[19] http://getfirebug.com/

[20] http://chrispederick.com/work/web-developer/

Chapter 3

Write Your Own Component

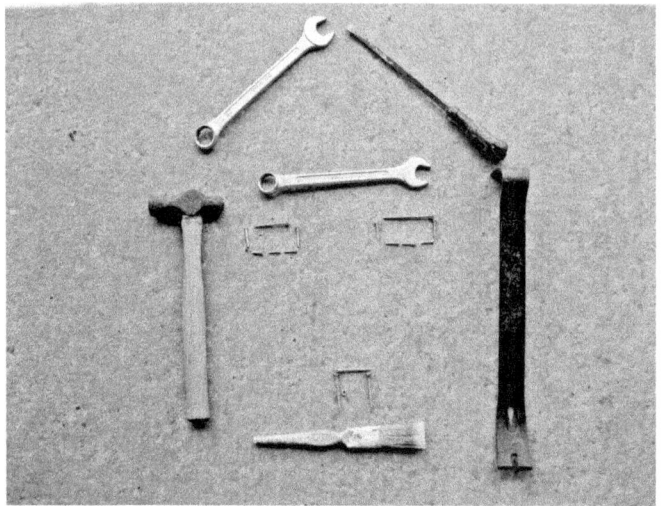

Photo: http://www.flickr.com/photos/59937401@N07/5857777188/ (CC BY 2.0)

Writing a component from scratch is hard work. Usually people that build websites with Joomla! search the Joomla! extension directory for existing components that fit their needs and usually they find something useful.

If not, they have to hire someone to write a component for their special needs or do it by themselves.

In this chapter we want to build a component for a real estate agency. It should contain house listings and detailed descriptions of the houses on the frontpage and a possibility to manage these listing in the backend. We have to think about the fields, the permissions, the image upload and many other requirements, too.

A typical Joomla! component like the web links component consists of 30+ files for the frontend and 30+ files for the backend. Every page in a Joomla! website contains the output of exactly one component.

MODEL-VIEW-CONTROLLER ARCHITECTURE

Joomla! is build on the model-view-controller architecture (MVC) which was first described for user interfaces of a programming language called Smalltalk in 1979.

Today MVC is the de facto standard in software development.

It comes in different flavours, control flow is generally as follows:

- The user interacts with the user interface in some way (for example, by clicking a submit button).

- The controller handles the event from the user interface, and converts it into an appropriate user action, understandable for the model.

- The controller notifies the model of the user action, possibly resulting in a change in the model's state. (For example, the controller updates the user's house listing.)

- A view queries the model in order to generate an appropriate user interface (for example, the view lists the house listings). The view gets its own data from the model.

- The user interface waits for further user interactions, which restarts the control flow cycle.

Joomla! MVC Implementation

In Joomla!, the MVC pattern is implemented using three classes: JModel, JView and JController. You can watch a good introduction to MCV by Andrew Eddy on YouTube[21].

Is It Necessary to Build A Component From Scratch?

A few years ago, building a component from scratch was the only way to enhance Joomla! core. Today we have several content construction kit components (CCK) available[22]. After installing one of these CCK components, you are able to configure additional content types with additional fields. The configuration is mostly easy but you depend on an additional Joomla! component that is the base of your use case.

> *I am a user and I want a simple directory for my website.*

Don't waste time with developing the component, download a CCK component and configure what you need.

> *I am a company with a use case that will not change in the next five years and I haven't found the right component in the JED. The company **has no** IT department with developers.*

Try to solve your problem with a CCK component. If it doesn't work, start with your own component.

> *I am a company with a use case that will not change in the next five years and I haven't found the right component in the JED. The company **has an** IT department with developers.*

Let the IT department come together and discuss it. Try out CCK components and individual component development.

> *I am a developer and I want to create components. I want to sell them online.*

Well, you have to learn it :)

How to Start?

---

[21] http://www.youtube.com/watch?v=BpZJpl2rf0U

[22] http://extensions.joomla.org/extensions/news-production/content-construction

I did a little research using Google, Joomla.org and the usual suspects. I found two very detailed tutorials on How to write an MVC component. The first one is from Christophe Demko, France [23], and the second one is from Rune V. Sjøen, Norway[24]. There are more tutorials available.

Another interesting approach for component development is to create a whole component automatically, based on your desires.

- A project on GitHub called jFoobar[25] started by Amy Stephen:

   JFoobar Component Builder builds a fully functioning Joomla Component, complete with ACL, Views, Models, and Controllers for the Administrator and Site. You can customise your Component for your site building needs by defining new data and customising the Layouts.

- A company called Not Web Design™ offers a component creator[26] as a paid service that will create all the necessary files based on your desired configuration. By using the paid pro version, you can create your own list and form views with custom fields, potentially saving you several days of work.

Try to build your own component from scratch to get an idea and afterwards try out both builders to check whether they are useful for you.

THE COCOATE REAL ESTATE COMPONENT

Based on the tutorials mentioned above, I will build a Real Estate component in *I am not sure right now how many* steps.

We need more or less three types of applications in one component.

- **Site**

   The site application, also called frontend, is the area of your site that guests and users see. It is used for displaying content. The components of the site application live in the */components* folder in your Joomla! root.

- **Administrator**

   The administrator application, also called backend, is the administration area of your site. Where logged in managers and administrators can manage the site. The components of the administrator application live in the */administrator/components* folder in your Joomla! root.

- **Installation and Update**

   To install an update for your component, we need *xml* files for configuration and meta data, sql files with database queries and, later on, an update server to provide new versions of the component.

---

[23] http://docs.joomla.org/Developing_a_Model-View-
Controller_(MVC)_Component_for_Joomla!1.6

[24] http://docs.joomla.org/User:Rvsjoen/tutorial/Developing_an_MVC_Component

[25] https://github.com/Niambie/jfoobar

[26] http://www.notwebdesign.com/joomla-component-creator

Chapter 4

Step 1 - The Basics

Photo: http://www.flickr.com/photos/22280677@N07/2994098078 (CC BY 2.0)

Let's collect a few facts about the first step to our Real Estate component. A component has to have a unique name and the easiest way to achieve that is to use your name or your company's name in the beginning.

- The human readable name for the component is **"Cocoate Real Estate"**.

- The machine readable name for the component is **cocoaterealestate** (While writing this component example I learned that it is better to avoid underscores in file names).

- The folders the component lives in are called **com_cocoaterealestate**

- It has one view called **object**. This view should display listings of houses later on.

- We need the possibility of creating a menu item to access the component

- We want to have a menu item in the backend that displays *coming soon*.

FRONTEND AND BACKEND

In "extension speech" the frontend is called **site** and the backend is called admin.

If you have a menu item on your page that leads to your component and a user clicks on this link,

- Joomla! evaluates the URL path: */index.php?option=com_cocoaterealestate*
- It searches the database components table for a component called *cocoaterealestate*.
- It looks for a folder called *com_cocoaterealestate* in the **site** folder components.
- In this folder it looks for a file called *cocoaterealestate.php*.
- It interprets this file.

The same happens in the **admin** area. If a manager or an administrator clicks the menu item,

- Joomla! evaluates the URL path: */administrator/index.php?option=com_cocoaterealestate*
- It searches the database components table for a component called *cocoaterealestate*.
- It looks for a folder called *com_cocoaterealestate* in the **site** folder components.
- In this folder it looks for a file called *cocoaterealestate.php*.
- It interprets this file.

Because we have to build two applications in one component with the same name, we have to have a structure. To interpret in the right way, you need several files.

- *cocoaterealestate.xml* – The XML file with all the information for the installer
- *cocoaterealestate.php* – The starting point of your component
- *controller.php* – The C in MVC, the controller
- *views/object/view.html.php* – The file which gets the data from the model (the M in MVC) and prepares it for the view (the V in MVC)
- *views/object/tmpl/default.php* – A default template for the component area of the page. It is possible to override this default template with the installed Joomla! template.

We need the same structure in the **admin** interface. Both applications are totally separate.

FILES AND INSTALLATION

Each extension needs a record in the extension table of the database. Without this record it doesn't exist in the "eyes" of the Joomla! CMS and it is not possible to use the extension, even when all files are in the right place. The database record will usually be created when you install the component.

But how to start. You have to write the component first :)

As always you have two possibilities.

DISCOVER EXTENSION

Since Joomla! 1.6 there is a discover option in the Extension Manager. You can place the files of your component in the right folders and click the discover option in the extension manager. It will read the components .xml file and update the extension table. The component is ready to use.

Your files should be placed like this. A file *index.html* has to be placed in each folder for security reasons.

```
/component/com_cocoaterealestate/cocoaterealestate.php
/component/com_cocoaterealestate/controller.php
/component/com_cocoaterealestate/index.html
/component/com_cocoaterealestate/view/object/view.html.php
```

```
/component/com_cocoaterealestate/view/object/index.html
/component/com_cocoaterealestate/view/object/tmpl/default.php
/component/com_cocoaterealestate/view/object/tmpl/default.xml
/component/com_cocoaterealestate/view/object/tmpl/index.html
/component/com_cocoaterealestate/view/index.html
/administrator/components/com_cocoaterealestate/cocoaterealestate.php
/administrator/components/com_cocoaterealestate/cocoaterealestate.xml
/administrator/components/com_cocoaterealestate/index.html
```

INSTALL EXTENSION

The other way is to install your extension via the Joomla! Extension Manager. In this case you have to place the files outside of Joomla!, compress them to a zip archive and upload it to the installer. After installation, the component is ready to use.

Your files should be placed like this. A file index.html has to be placed in each folder for security reasons.

```
/site/cocoaterealestate.php
/site/controller.php
/site/index.html
/site/view/object/view.html.php
/site/view/object/index.html
/site/view/object/tmpl/default.php
/site/view/object/tmpl/default.xml
/site/view/object/tmpl/index.html
/site/view/index.html
/administrator/cocoaterealestate.php
/administrator/cocoaterealestate.xml
/administrator/index.html
```

You find the example component for download on our website[27].

THE CODE

In total we need 7 files with code and the index.html file.

File: index.html

If a visitor navigates his browser directly to a folder of the component, it would be possible, depending on the configuration of the web server, that he would see a directory of that folder. To avoid that you have to place a file called index.html in each folder (Listing 1). This requirement is a moot point (The files of wrath[28]) but it is still necessary to get listed in the Joomla! Extension Directory.

```
<!DOCTYPE html><title></title>
```

Listing 1: index.html

File: /administrator/cocoaterealestate.php

---

[27] http://cocoate.com/jdev/component/step-1

[28] http://www.dionysopoulos.me/blog/the-files-of-wrath

This is the file, which is executed when you click the component in the administration area (*Figure 1*). It can contain "everything" :)

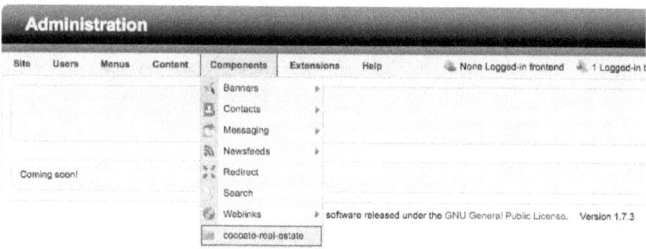

Figure 1: Output in Backend

```
Coming soon!
```

Listing 2: /administrator/cocoaterealestate.php

File: /administrator/cocoaterealestate.xml

The *.xml* file contains meta data and the information where to put the files. You can see parts of the data in Figure 2.

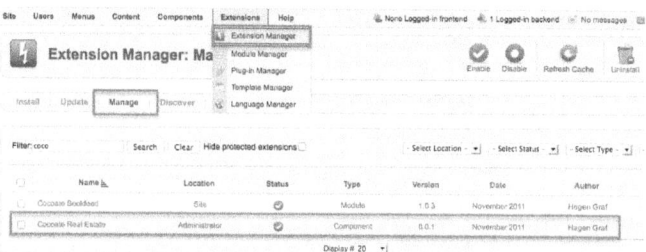

Figure 2: XML Data in Extension Manager

```
<?xml version="1.0" encoding="utf-8"?>

<extension type="component" version="1.7.0" method="upgrade">

    <name>Cocoate Real Estate</name>
        <!-- The following elements are optional and free of formatting
constraints -->
    <creationDate>November 2011</creationDate>
    <author>Hagen Graf</author>
    <authorEmail>hagen@cocoate.com</authorEmail>
    <authorUrl>http://cocoate.com</authorUrl>
    <copyright>2006-2011 cocoate.com - All rights reserved</copyright>
```

```
<license>GPL 2</license>
<!--  The version string is stored in the components table -->
<version>0.0.1</version>
<!-- The description is optional and defaults to the name -->
<description>House listings on your website.</description>

<!-- Note the folder attribute: This attribute describes the folder
     to copy FROM in the package to install therefore files copied
     in this section are copied from "site/" in the package -->
<files folder="site">
    <filename>index.html</filename>
    <filename>cocoaterealestate.php</filename>
    <filename>controller.php</filename>
    <folder>views</folder>
</files>

<administration>
    <menu>Cocoate Real Estate</menu>
    <!-- Note the folder attribute: This attribute describes the folder
         to copy FROM in the package to install therefore files copied
         in this section are copied from "admin/" in the package -->
    <files folder="admin">
        <filename>index.html</filename>
        <filename>cocoaterealestate.php</filename>
    </files>
</administration>
</extension>
```

Listing 3: /administrator/cocoaterealestate.xml

File: /site/cocoaterealestate.php

The defined ('_JEXEC') or die; statement has to be for security reasons at the top of each .php file. This statement checks to see if the file is being called from within a Joomla! session (*Listing 4*).

```
// No direct access to this file
defined('_JEXEC') or die;

// Import of the necessary classes
jimport('joomla.application.component.controller');

// Get an instance of the controller prefixed by CocoateRealEstate
$controller = JController::getInstance('CocoateRealEstate');
```

```
// Perform the Request task
$controller->execute(JRequest::getCmd('task'));


// Redirect if set by the controller
$controller->redirect();
```

Listing 4: /site/cocoaterealestate.php

File: /site/controller.php

This is the controller, the C of MVC. At the moment there is nothing to control, so the file remains empty (*Listing 5*)

```
defined('_JEXEC') or die;

jimport('joomla.application.component.controller');

class CocoateRealEstateController extends JController
{
}
```

Listing 5: /site/controller.php

File: /site/view/object/view.html.php

Views are the V in MVC and they are separated in various views. The name of the folder is the name of the view. In our case we'll need a listing of all houses and a detailed page for one object. The views are separated in files for collecting the necessary data from the model (which will come later too) and the template file with the markup. In Listing 4 you see the data collection for the objects list.

```
// No direct access to this file

defined('_JEXEC') or die;

jimport('joomla.application.component.view');

class CocoateRealEstateViewObject extends JView
{

    function display($tpl = null)

    {

        // Assign data to the view
        $this->item = 'Cocoate Real Estate';


        // Display the view
        parent::display($tpl);

    }

}
```

Listing 6: /site/view/object/view.html.php

File: /site/view/object/tmpl/default.php

This is the template file with the markup (Listing 7). This file can be copied to and overwritten by the main Joomla! template.

```
// No direct access to this file

defined('_JEXEC') or die;
```

```
?>
<h1><?php echo $this->item; ?></h1>
```

Listing 7: /site/view/object/tmpl/default.php

File: /site/view/object/tmpl/default.xml

This is the configuration file for the menu item Manager *(Figure 3, Listing 8)*

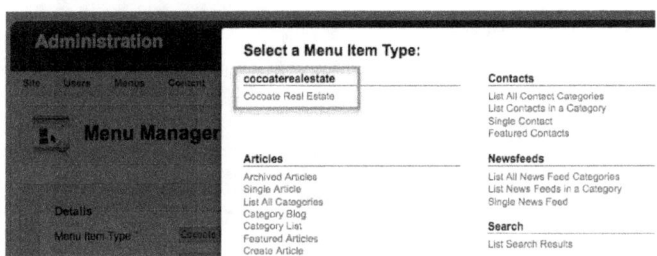

Figure 3: XML Data in Menu Manager

```xml
<?xml version="1.0" encoding="utf-8"?>
<metadata>
  <layout title="Cocoate Real Estate">
    <message>Object</message>
  </layout>
</metadata>
```

Listing 8: /site/view/object/tmpl/default.xml

Chapter 5

Step 2 - Database, Backend, Languages

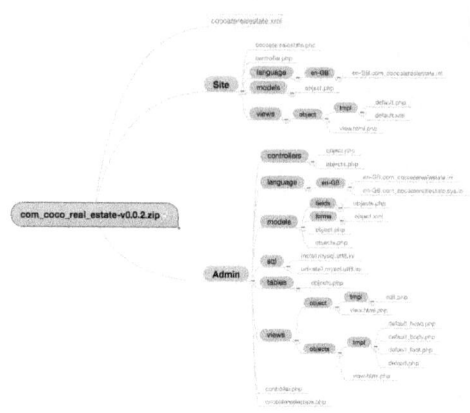

After the basics we want to achieve more.

We want to have a fully functioning component with a backend for adding, editing and deleting objects and we want to have separated language files, of course, to have the possibility to localise our component. In general this is not complicated but we have to create many files and it is easy to get lost in folders, filenames and methods.

I want you to start with a few screenshots to give you an idea of what I am talking about :)

COCOATE REAL ESTATE (CRE) VERSION 0.0.2 SCREENSHOTS

The component consists more or less of two components. One is responsible for the Frontend (site) and one for the administration area (admin). It is still a simple component without eye candy, ACL, additional JavaScript and all the other fancy stuff but it will be a robust foundation to discover more.

Site

For the moment we only want to have the possibility to create a link to one object (*Figure 1*). Later on we will enhance that.

Figure 1: One listing in the frontend

Admin

To be able to create the menu link for the site we need a menu item type (*Figure 2*).

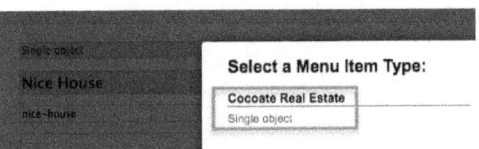

Figure 2: Menu Item Type

After we choose the menu item Type we have to select the object we want to present. There will be an option list consisting of different fields fetched from the database. This step is important because in our first try we just wrote the text in an xml file. Here the option list is created dynamically, depending on the content of our database table (*Figure 3*).

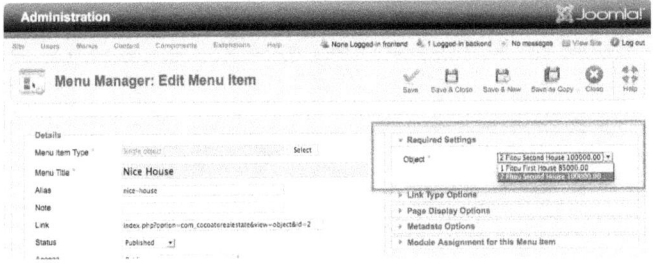

Figure 3: Dynamic Parameters

To add, edit and delete objects we need an overview page like in *Figure 4*. We need a headline, a toolbar with Icons, checkboxes and of course content.

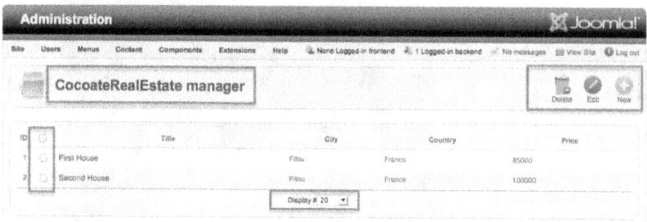

Figure 4: Backend Table

When you click on the title link you should be directed to an edit form. In this edit form, we need a different toolbar, fields and of course labels and description to help the user to understand what should be done (*Figure 5*). The form should appear, too, when the *New* icon is clicked! After saving, there should be a message for the user.

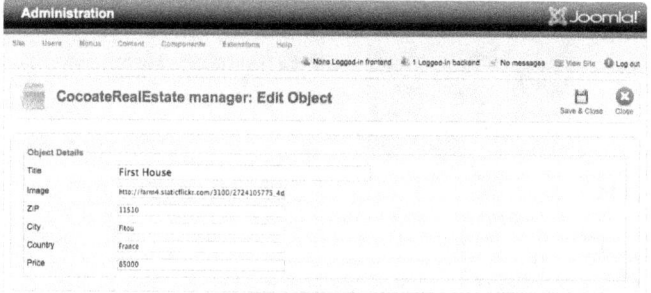

Figure 5: Edit Form

In the case of edit, it should be possible to tick the checkbox of the row and click the icon edit. If nothing is checked and the edit icon is clicked there should be a message (*Figure 6*)

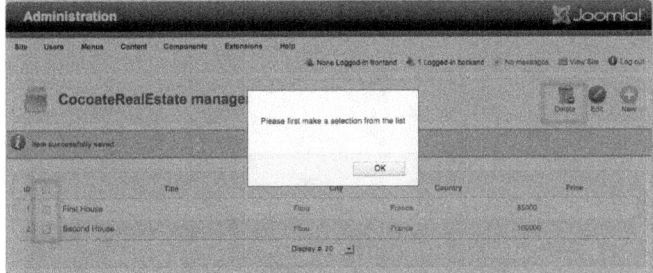

Figure 6: Message that Nothing Is Checked

And last but not least, it should be possible to delete the freshly added object.

CRE VERSION 0.0.2 FILES

In this step we need a lot of additional files. If you still work with a "simple" text editor it can become a bit confusing. I propose that you install the example component[29] and go through all the files.

It is important to keep in mind that the folder structure in the installation package differs from the folder structure in the Joomla! CMS.

Please take your time and have a look at the folder structure in the ZIP file (*Figure 7*) and the file structure in the CMS after installing (*Figure 8*).

---

[29] http://cocoate.com/jdev/component/step-2 at the bottom of the chapter

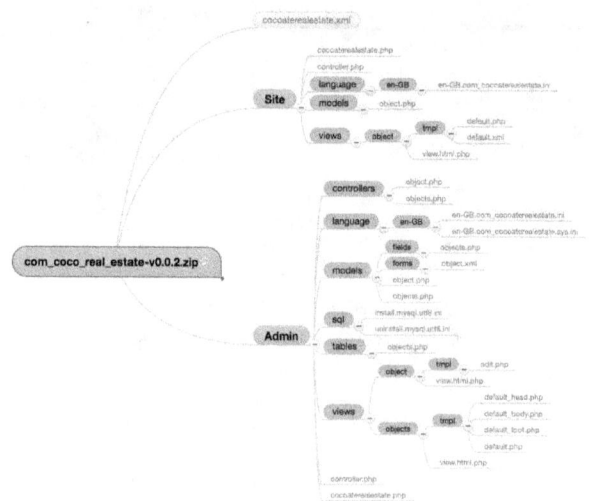

Figure 7: Folder Structure in Installation Package

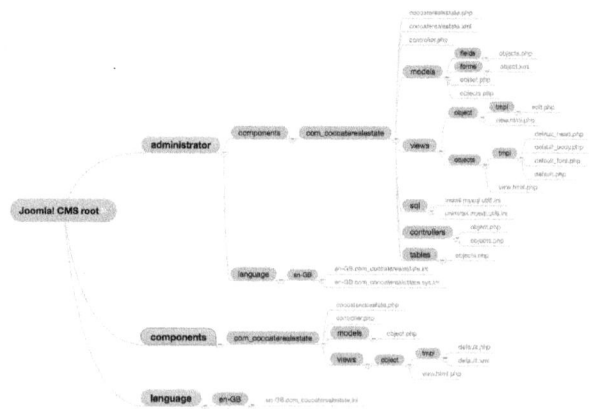

Figure 8: Folder Structure in Joomla! CMS

DATABASE TABLE COCOATEREALESTATE_OBJECTS

We need to store our listings somewhere and I had a chicken and egg[30] problem when I wrote the chapter. Of course I wrote two files for installing and uninstalling the table *cocoaterealestate_objects* (*Listing 1, Listing 2*) but initially I built the table manually using phpMyAdmin.

After the code was complete, it was possible to install the component and the two files are executed from the installing and uninstalling process.

The files contain pure SQL commands and consequently the extension is .sql. To keep it "simple" I structured the table in a simple way with fields for title, image, description, city, zip, country and price. Keep in mind that the drop command at the top of the install file can accidentally delete existing data. Depending on your update plans it can be useful or dangerous :).

```
DROP TABLE IF EXISTS `#__cocoaterealestate_objects`;


CREATE TABLE `#__cocoaterealestate_objects` (
  `id` int(10) unsigned NOT NULL AUTO_INCREMENT,
  `uid` int(10) unsigned NOT NULL DEFAULT '0',
  `created` timestamp NOT NULL DEFAULT CURRENT_TIMESTAMP,
  `published` tinyint(1) unsigned NOT NULL DEFAULT '0',
  `ordering` int(10) unsigned NOT NULL DEFAULT '0',
  `image` varchar(255)  NOT NULL DEFAULT '',
  `meta_descr` varchar(250) DEFAULT NULL,
  `meta_keys` varchar(250) DEFAULT NULL,
  `title` varchar(200) NOT NULL DEFAULT '',
  `description` text,
  `city` varchar(100) NOT NULL DEFAULT '',
  `zip` varchar(50) NOT NULL DEFAULT '',
  `country` varchar(100) NOT NULL DEFAULT '',
  `price` int(10) NOT NULL DEFAULT '0',
  PRIMARY KEY (`id`)
) ENGINE=MyISAM  DEFAULT CHARSET=utf8 AUTO_INCREMENT=3 ;


INSERT INTO `#__cocoaterealestate_objects`  VALUES(1, 42, '2011-11-29
15:39:10',   1,   0,   'http://farm4.staticflickr.com/
3100/2724105775_4d039b4127.jpg', NULL, NULL, 'First House', 'Sed id leo
metus, ut mollis mi. Etiam malesuada ornare felis, vel imperdiet eros cursus
sollicitudin. Nulla viverra, neque sodales porttitor accumsan, felis purus
varius libero, eu posuere odio risus ac nisl. Proin quis eros ipsum, sit
amet pretium eros? Proin at purus cras amet.\r\n', 'Fitou', '11510',
'France', 85000);


INSERT INTO `#__cocoaterealestate_objects` VALUES(2, 42, '2011-11-29
15:39:10',   1,   0,   'http://farm6.staticflickr.com/
5298/5489897350_eaf091d99b.jpg', NULL, NULL, 'Second House', 'bumsclabe
laber Sed id leo metus, ut mollis mi. Etiam malesuada ornare felis, vel
```

---

[30] http://en.wikipedia.org/wiki/Chicken_or_the_egg

```
imperdiet eros cursus sollicitudin. Nulla viverra, neque sodales porttitor
accumsan, felis purus varius libero, eu posuere odio risus ac nisl. Proin
quis eros ipsum, sit amet pretium eros? Proin at purus cras amet.\r\n',
'Fitou', '11510', 'France', 100000);
```

Listing 1: /administrator/components/com_cocoaterealestate/sql/install.mysql.utf8.sql

```
DROP TABLE IF EXISTS `#__cocoaterealestate_objects`;
```

Listing 2: /administrator/components/com_cocoaterealestate/sql/uninstall.mysql.utf8.sql

MODELS, TABLES, FIELDS, LANGUAGE FILES

Besides the database table itself, we need a table class and various models to manage the needs of our component.

Table Class

The table class lives in the administration area of the CMS in */administrator/components/ com_cocoate_realestate/tables/objects.php* (*Listing 3*). You define as many tables as you need. The name of the class consists of a prefix (*CocoateRealEstateTable*) and of the virtual name of the table (Objects). An instance of this class represents a row in the db table which means one house listing.

```php
<?php
// No direct access to this file
defined('_JEXEC') or die;
jimport('joomla.database.table');
class CocoateRealEstateTableObjects extends JTable
{
  var $id = null;
  var $title = null;
  var $city = null;
  var $price = null;
  var $published = 0;

  function __construct(&$db)
  {
    parent::__construct('#__cocoaterealestate_objects', 'id', $db);
  }
}
?>
```

Listing 3: /administrator/components/com_cocoate_realestate/tables/objects.php

Model - Frontend

The cool thing is that we can create a link for a single object (*Figure 1*). Therefore we need a model for ONE row (one object/house listing). It is important to distinguish between a single house listing and list/table of house listings. In Joomla! we call the model file in a singular way, if we want to have ONE item (*object.php*) and in the plural way if we want a list of items (*objects.php*). The name of the model has to be similar to the name of the view folder.

In our case the name of the view folder is object so we call the model file object.php too (*Listing 4*).

```php
<?php
// No direct access to this file
defined('_JEXEC') or die('Restricted access');
jimport('joomla.application.component.modelitem');
class CocoateRealEstateModelObject extends JModelItem
{
  protected $item;
  public function getItem()
  {
    if (!isset($this->item)) {
      $id = JRequest::getInt('id');
      // Get a TableObject instance
      $table = $this->getTable('Objects', 'CocoateRealEstateTable');
      // Load the object
      $table->load($id);
      // Assign the data
      $this->item['id'] = $table->id;
      $this->item['image'] = $table->image;
      $this->item['title'] = $table->title;
      $this->item['city'] = $table->city;
      $this->item['zip'] = $table->zip;
      $this->item['country'] = $table->country;
      $this->item['price'] = $table->price;
    }
    return $this->item;
  }
}
?>
```

Listing 4: /components/com_cocoate_realestate/models/object.php

Model/Field - Backend

The view related to the object model needs a kind of relationship to this model. This is done by an entry in an xml file called */components/cocoaterealestate/views/object/tmpl/default.xml (Listing 5)*. The important attribute is addfieldpath. The WORDS IN CAPITAL LETTERS are variables for language files.

```xml
<?xml version="1.0" encoding="utf-8"?>
<metadata>
  <layout title="COM_COCOATEREALESTATE_OBJECT_VIEW_DEFAULT_TITLE">
    <message>COM_COCOATEREALESTATE_OBJECT_VIEW_DEFAULT_DESC</message>
  </layout>
```

```
    <fields name="request" addfieldpath="/administrator/components/
com_cocoaterealestate/models/fields">
      <fieldset name="request">
        <field
          name="id"
          type="object"
          extension="com_cocoaterealestate"
          label="COM_COCOATEREALESTATE_OBJECT_FIELD_OBJECT_LABEL"
          description="COM_COCOATEREALESTATE_OBJECT_FIELD_OBJECT_LABEL"
          required="true"
          />
      </fieldset>
    </fields>
  </metadata>
```

Listing 5: /components/cocoaterealestate/views/object/tmpl/default.xml

Language Files

Language files have nothing to do with models but I want to mention them now because we need them and I already have used language variables (THE ONES WITH CAPITAL LETTERS).

The language file for the frontend would be */language/en-GB/en-GB.com_cocoaterealestate.ini*. The name for the German language file would be */language/de-DE/de-DE.com_cocoaterealestate.ini*. At the moment we need no text strings for the frontend.

The two language files for the backend are stored in the folder */administrator/language/en-GB/*. One is called *en-GB.com_cocoaterealestate.sys.ini* (*Listing 6*) and the other one is called *en-GB.com_cocoaterealestate.ini* (*Listing 7*). The *sys.ini* file will be used during the installation process, in the extension manager and in the menus. It contains a lot less translation strings and this file is loaded in scenarios where the loaded component is not *com_cocoaterealestate* itself, but minimal translation is still needed.

```
COM_COCOATEREALESTATE="Cocoate Real Estate"
COM_COCOATEREALESTATE_DESCRIPTION="House listings on your website."
COM_COCOATEREALESTATE_OBJECT_VIEW_DEFAULT_TITLE="Single object"
COM_COCOATEREALESTATE_OBJECT_VIEW_DEFAULT_DESC="This view displays a single object"
COM_COCOATEREALESTATE_MENU="Cocoate Real Estate"
```

Listing 6: /administratorlanguage/en-GB/en-GB.com_cocoaterealestate.sys.ini

```
COM_COCOATEREALESTATE_OBJECT_FIELD_OBJECT_DESC="This object will be displayed"
COM_COCOATEREALESTATE_OBJECT_FIELD_OBJECT_LABEL="Object"
COM_COCOATEREALESTATE_OBJECT_HEADING_ID="ID"
COM_COCOATEREALESTATE_OBJECT_HEADING_OBJECT="Object"
COM_COCOATEREALESTATE_OBJECT_HEADING_TITLE="Title"
COM_COCOATEREALESTATE_OBJECT_HEADING_COUNTRY="Country"
COM_COCOATEREALESTATE_OBJECT_HEADING_CITY="City"
```

```
COM_COCOATEREALESTATE_OBJECT_HEADING_IMAGE="Image"
COM_COCOATEREALESTATE_OBJECT_HEADING_ZIP="ZIP"
COM_COCOATEREALESTATE_OBJECT_HEADING_PRICE="Price"
COM_COCOATEREALESTATE_MANAGER_OBJECTS="CocoateRealEstate manager"
COM_COCOATEREALESTATE_MANAGER_OBJECT_NEW="CocoateRealEstate  manager:  New
Object"
COM_COCOATEREALESTATE_MANAGER_OBJECT_EDIT="CocoateRealEstate  manager:  Edit
Object"
COM_COCOATEREALESTATE_N_ITEMS_DELETED_1="One object deleted"
COM_COCOATEREALESTATE_N_ITEMS_DELETED_MORE="%d objects deleted"
COM_COCOATEREALESTATE_OBJECT_DETAILS="Object Details"
COM_COCOATEREALESTATE_OBJECT_FIELD_TITLE_LABEL="Title"
COM_COCOATEREALESTATE_OBJECT_FIELD_TITLE_DESC="Title"
COM_COCOATEREALESTATE_OBJECT_FIELD_IMAGE_LABEL="Image"
COM_COCOATEREALESTATE_OBJECT_FIELD_IMAGE_DESC="Please paste a URL"
COM_COCOATEREALESTATE_OBJECT_FIELD_ZIP_LABEL="ZIP"
COM_COCOATEREALESTATE_OBJECT_FIELD_ZIP_DESC="Enter ZIP code"
COM_COCOATEREALESTATE_OBJECT_FIELD_CITY_LABEL="City"
COM_COCOATEREALESTATE_OBJECT_FIELD_CITY_DESC="City"
COM_COCOATEREALESTATE_OBJECT_FIELD_COUNTRY_LABEL="Country"
COM_COCOATEREALESTATE_OBJECT_FIELD_COUNTRY_DESC="Country"
COM_COCOATEREALESTATE_OBJECT_FIELD_PRICE_LABEL="Price"
COM_COCOATEREALESTATE_OBJECT_FIELD_PRICE_DESC="Enter price"
```

Listing 7: /administratorlanguage/en-GB/en-GB.com_cocoaterealestate.ini

Models, Fields and Forms - Backend

The parameter field for choosing the right object for the menu link needs a relationship to the model. Therefore we create a folder fields inside of the models folder. In this folder we store the structure of the parameter field and call it *object.php* (*Listing 8*).

```php
<?php
defined('_JEXEC') or die;
jimport('joomla.form.helper');
JFormHelper::loadFieldClass('list');
class JFormFieldObject extends JFormFieldList
{
  protected $type = 'Object';
  protected function getOptions()
  {
    $db = JFactory::getDBO();
    $query = $db->getQuery(true);
    $query->select('id,title,price,city');
    $query->from('#__cocoaterealestate_objects');
    $db->setQuery((string)$query);
```

```
$titles = $db->loadObjectList();
$options = array();
if($titles){
    foreach($titles as $title)
    {
        $options[] = JHtml::_('select.option', $title->id, $title->id.' '.
$title->city.' '.$title->title.' '.money_format('%i', $title->price));
    }
}
$options = array_merge(parent::getOptions(), $options);
return $options;
}
}
```

Listing 8: /administrator/components/com_cocoate_realestate/models/fields/object.php

In the backend, we have an overview page (*Figure 4*) and a form for editing and adding a single object (*Figure 5*). For that reason we need two models - *object.php* and *objects.php* (*Listing 9 and Listing 10*)

```
<?php
// No direct access to this file
defined('_JEXEC') or die;
jimport('joomla.application.component.modeladmin');
class CocoateRealEstateModelObject extends JModelAdmin
{
    public function getForm($data = array(), $loadData = true)
    {
        // Get the form.
        $form = $this->loadForm('com_cocoaterealestate.object', 'object',
array('control' => 'jform', 'load_data' => $loadData));
        return $form;
    }


    protected function loadFormData()
    {
        // Check the session for previously entered form data.
        $data = JFactory::getApplication()-
>getUserState('com_cocoaterealestate.edit.object.data', array());
        if(empty($data)){
            $data = $this->getItem();
        }
        return $data;
    }
```

```
   public function getTable($name = 'Objects', $prefix =
'CocoateRealEstateTable', $options = array())
  {
    return parent::getTable($name, $prefix, $options);
  }
}
```

Listing 9: /administrator/components/com_cocoate_realestate/models/object.php

```php
<?php
// No direct access to this file
defined('_JEXEC') or die;
jimport('joomla.application.component.modellist');
class CocoateRealEstateModelObjects extends JModelList
{
  protected function getListQuery()
  {
    // Create a new query object.
    $db = JFactory::getDBO();
    $query = $db->getQuery(true);

    // Select some fields
    $query->select('id,title,city,country,price');

    // From the realestate table
    $query->from('#__cocoaterealestate_objects');
    return $query;
  }
}
?>
```

Listing 10: /administrator/components/com_cocoate_realestate/models/objects.php

To add an object/listing we need a form. Forms are located in the model folder, too. The extension for form files is .xml and the name is the same as the name of the view where the form is needed. In our case, the name is again objects (*Listing 11*).

```xml
<?xml version="1.0" encoding="utf-8"?>
<form>
  <fieldset>
    <field
      name="id"
      type="hidden"
    />
    <field
      name="title"
      type="text"
```

```
    label="COM_COCOATEREALESTATE_OBJECT_FIELD_TITLE_LABEL"
    description="COM_COCOATEREALESTATE_OBJECT_FIELD_TITLE_DESC"
    size="40"
    class="inputbox"
    default=""
/>
<field
  name="image"
  type="text"
  label="COM_COCOATEREALESTATE_OBJECT_FIELD_IMAGE_LABEL"
  description="COM_COCOATEREALESTATE_OBJECT_FIELD_IMAGE_DESC"
  size="40"
  class="inputbox"
  default=""
/>
<field
  name="zip"
  type="text"
  label="COM_COCOATEREALESTATE_OBJECT_FIELD_ZIP_LABEL"
  description="COM_COCOATEREALESTATE_OBJECT_FIELD_ZIP_DESC"
  size="40"
  class="inputbox"
  default=""
/>
<field
  name="city"
  type="text"
  label="COM_COCOATEREALESTATE_OBJECT_FIELD_CITY_LABEL"
  description="COM_COCOATEREALESTATE_OBJECT_FIELD_CITY_DESC"
  size="40"
  class="inputbox"
  default=""
/>
<field
  name="country"
  type="text"
  label="COM_COCOATEREALESTATE_OBJECT_FIELD_COUNTRY_LABEL"
  description="COM_COCOATEREALESTATE_OBJECT_FIELD_COUNTRY_DESC"
  size="40"
  class="inputbox"
  default=""
```

```
    />
    <field
      name="price"
      type="text"
      label="COM_COCOATEREALESTATE_OBJECT_FIELD_PRICE_LABEL"
      description="COM_COCOATEREALESTATE_OBJECT_FIELD_PRICE_DESC"
      size="40"
      class="inputbox"
      default=""
    />
  </fieldset>
</form>
```

Listing 11: /administrator/components/com_cocoate_realestate/models/forms/objects.xml

CONTROLLERS

The controllers are necessary to be able to decide what to do next. If you click the "*New*" icon to add a house listing, a controller has to find the right way what to do next. In total we use four controllers at the moment.

- One for the frontend (*/component/com_cocoaterealestate/controller.php - listing 12*)
- One generic controller with a default option (in our case objects) for the backend (*/administrator/component/com_cocoaterealestate/controller.php - listing 13*)
- Two controllers for the backend for the list view (*/administrator/component/com_cocoaterealestate/controllers/objects.php - listing 14*) and for the single view (*/administrator/component/com_cocoaterealestate/controllers/object.php - listing 15*).

/component/com_cocoaterealestate/controller.php

This controller does nothing at the moment. It simply has to be there (*Listing 12*).

```
<?php
// No direct access to this file
defined('_JEXEC') or die;
jimport('joomla.application.component.controller');
class CocoateRealEstateController extends JController
{
}
```

Listing 12: /administrator/component/com_cocoaterealestate/controller.php

/administrator/component/com_cocoaterealestate/controller.php

The controller has to be there, too, but in this case we have two views, so one of must be the default view. The controller sets the default view to objects.

```
<?php
// No direct access to this file
defined('_JEXEC') or die;
jimport('joomla.application.component.controller');
class CocoateRealEstateController extends JController
```

```
{
  function display($cachable = false)
  {
    // Set default view if not set
    JRequest::setVar('view', JRequest::getCmd('view', 'objects'));
    parent::display($cachable);
  }
}
?>
```

Listing 13: /administrator/component/com_cocoaterealestate/controller.php

administrator/component/com_cocoaterealestate/controllers/objects.php

```
<?php
// No direct access to this file
defined('_JEXEC') or die;
jimport('joomla.application.component.controlleradmin');
class CocoateRealEstateControllerObjects extends JControllerAdmin
{
    public function getModel($name = 'Object', $prefix =
'CocoateRealEstateModel')          {
        $model = parent::getModel($name, $prefix, array('ignore_request' =>
true));
        return $model;
    }
}
```

Listing 14 /administrator/component/com_cocoaterealestate/controllers/objects.php

administrator/component/com_cocoaterealestate/controllers/object.php
This controller has to be there but can remain empty.

```
<?php
// No direct access to this file
defined('_JEXEC') or die;
jimport('joomla.application.component.controllerform');
class CocoateRealEstateControllerObject extends JControllerForm
{
}
```

Listing 15 /administrator/component/com_cocoaterealestate/controllers/object.php

VIEWS IN FRONTEND AND BACKEND
In our example we have three views:

The object view in the frontend (*Figure 1*) displaying a single object. It consists of three files:
/component/com_cocoaterealestate/views/object/view.html.php (Listing 16)
/component/com_cocoaterealestate/views/object/tmpl/default.php (Listing 17)

/component/com_cocoaterealestate/views/object/tmpl/default.xml (Listing 18) (I already mentioned that file above)

The objects view in the backend (*Figure 4*) displays a list of objects/houses. It consists of five files:
/administrator/component/com_cocoaterealestate/views/object/view.html.php (Listing 19)
/administrator/component/com_cocoaterealestate/views/object/tmpl/default.php (Listing 20)
/administrator/component/com_cocoaterealestate/views/object/tmpl/default_body.php (Listing 21)
/administrator/component/com_cocoaterealestate/views/object/tmpl/default_foot.php (Listing 22)
/administrator/component/com_cocoaterealestate/views/object/tmpl/default_head.php (Listing 23)

The object view in the backend (Figure 5) displays the form. It consists of two files:
/administrator/component/com_cocoaterealestate/views/object/view.html.php (Listing 24)
/administrator/component/com_cocoaterealestate/views/object/tmpl/edit.php (Listing 25)

The structure of the views are very important. The view.html.php collects the data from the model and provides it as variables for the "real" template called default.php. The default.php is made for designers and it is overridable by any Joomla! template (Read more in Chapter Template Overrides). It should contain only markup enriched with PHP variables.

```php
<?php
// No direct access to this file
defined('_JEXEC') or die;
jimport('joomla.application.component.view');
class CocoateRealEstateViewObject extends JView
{
  protected $item;
  function display($tpl = null)
  {
    // Assign data to the view
    //$this->item = 'Cocoate Real Estate';
    $this->item = $this->get('item');

    // Display the view
    parent::display($tpl);
  }
}
```

Listing 16: /component/com_cocoaterealestate/views/object/view.html.php

```php
<?php
// No direct access to this file
defined('_JEXEC') or die;
?>
<h1><?php echo $this->item['title']; ?></h1>
<img src="<?php echo $this->item['image']; ?>">
<ul>
  <li>
```

```php
<?php echo $this->item['zip']; ?>
<?php echo $this->item['city']; ?>,
<?php echo $this->item['country']; ?>
</li>
<li>
<strong><?php echo $this->item['price']; ?> €</strong>
</li>
</ul>
<pre>
<?php
// uncomment the next line to see the array
// print_r($this->item); ?>
</pre>
```

Listing 17: /component/com_cocoaterealestate/views/object/tmpl/default.php

```xml
<?xml version="1.0" encoding="utf-8"?>
<metadata>
  <layout title="COM_COCOATEREALESTATE_OBJECT_VIEW_DEFAULT_TITLE">
    <message>COM_COCOATEREALESTATE_OBJECT_VIEW_DEFAULT_DESC</message>
  </layout>
    <fields name="request" addfieldpath="/administrator/components/
com_cocoaterealestate/models/fields">
    <fieldset name="request">
      <field
        name="id"
        type="object"
        extension="com_cocoaterealestate"
        label="COM_COCOATEREALESTATE_OBJECT_FIELD_OBJECT_LABEL"
        description="COM_COCOATEREALESTATE_OBJECT_FIELD_OBJECT_LABEL"
        required="true"
        />
    </fieldset>
  </fields>
</metadata>
```

Listing 18: /component/com_cocoaterealestate/views/object/tmpl/default.xml

```php
<?php
// No direct access to this file
defined('_JEXEC') or die;
jimport('joomla.application.component.view');
class CocoateRealEstateViewObjects extends JView
{
  function display($tpl = null)
```

```php
  {
    // Get data from the model
    $items = $this->get('Items');
    $pagination = $this->get('Pagination');

    // Assign data to the view
    $this->items = $items;
    $this->pagination = $pagination;

    // Set the toolbar
    $this->addToolBar();

    // Display the template
    parent::display($tpl);
  }

  protected function addToolBar()
  {
JToolBarHelper::title(JText::_('COM_COCOATEREALESTATE_MANAGER_OBJECTS'));
    JToolBarHelper::deleteListX('', 'objects.delete');
    JToolBarHelper::editListX('object.edit');
    JToolBarHelper::addNewX('object.add');
  }
}
?>
```

Listing 19: /administrator/component/com_cocoaterealestate/views/object/view.html.php

```php
<?php
// No direct access to this file
defined('_JEXEC') or die;
JHtml::_('behavior.tooltip');
?>
<form action="<?php echo JRoute::_('index.php?option=com_cocoaterealestate'); ?>" method="post" name="adminForm">
  <table class="adminlist">
    <thead><?php echo $this->loadTemplate('head');?></thead>
    <tfoot><?php echo $this->loadTemplate('foot');?></tfoot>
    <tbody><?php echo $this->loadTemplate('body');?></tbody>
  </table>
  <div>
    <input type="hidden" name="task" value="" />
    <input type="hidden" name="boxchecked" value="0" />
```

```php
    <?php echo JHtml::_('form.token'); ?>
  </div>
</form>
```

Listing 20: /administrator/component/com_cocoaterealestate/views/object/tmpl/default.php

```php
<?php
// No direct access to this file
defined('_JEXEC') or die;
?>
<?php foreach($this->items as $i => $item): ?>
  <tr class="row<?php echo $i % 2; ?>">
    <td><?php echo $item->id; ?></td>
    <td><?php echo JHtml::_('grid.id', $i, $item->id); ?></td>
    <td>
        <a   href="<?php   echo   JRoute::_('index.php?
option=com_cocoaterealestate&task=object.edit&id=' . $item->id); ?>">
    <?php echo $item->title; ?>
    </a>
    </td>
    <td><?php echo $item->city; ?></td>
    <td><?php echo $item->country; ?></td>
    <td><?php echo $item->price; ?></td>
  </tr>
<?php endforeach; ?>
```

Listing 21: /administrator/component/com_cocoaterealestate/views/object/tmpl/default_body.php

```php
<?php
// No direct access to this file
defined('_JEXEC') or die;
?>
<tr>
  <td colspan="6"><?php echo $this->pagination->getListFooter(); ?></td>
</tr>
```

Listing 22: /administrator/component/com_cocoaterealestate/views/object/tmpl/default_foot.php

```php
<?php
// No direct access to this file
defined('_JEXEC') or die;
?>
<tr>
  <th width="5">
  <?php echo JText::_('COM_COCOATEREALESTATE_OBJECT_HEADING_ID'); ?>
  </th>
  <th width="20">
```

```
    <input type="checkbox" name="toggle" value="" onclick="checkAll(<?php echo
count($this->items); ?>);" />
    </th>
    <th>
    <?php echo JText::_('COM_COCOATEREALESTATE_OBJECT_HEADING_TITLE'); ?>
    </th>
    <th>
    <?php echo JText::_('COM_COCOATEREALESTATE_OBJECT_HEADING_CITY'); ?>
    </th>
    <th>
    <?php echo JText::_('COM_COCOATEREALESTATE_OBJECT_HEADING_COUNTRY'); ?>
    </th>
    <th>
    <?php echo JText::_('COM_COCOATEREALESTATE_OBJECT_HEADING_PRICE'); ?>
    </th>
</tr>
```

Listing 23: /administrator/component/com_cocoaterealestate/views/object/tmpl/default_head.php

```php
<?php
// No direct access to this file
defined('_JEXEC') or die;
jimport('joomla.application.component.view');
class CocoateRealEstateViewObject extends JView
{
  public function display($tpl = null)
  {
    // get the Data
    $form = $this->get('Form');
    $item = $this->get('Item');

    // Assign the Data
    $this->form = $form;
    $this->item = $item;

    // Set the toolbar
    $this->addToolBar();

    // Display the template
    parent::display($tpl);
  }

  protected function addToolBar()
  {
```

```
    JRequest::setVar('hidemainmenu', true);
    $isNew = ($this->item->id == 0);
                        JToolBarHelper::title($isNew      ?
JText::_('COM_COCOATEREALESTATE_MANAGER_OBJECT_NEW')    :
JText::_('COM_COCOATEREALESTATE_MANAGER_OBJECT_EDIT'));
    JToolBarHelper::save('object.save');
      JToolBarHelper::cancel('object.cancel', $isNew ? 'JTOOLBAR_CANCEL' :
'JTOOLBAR_CLOSE');
  }
}
```

Listing 24: /administrator/component/com_cocoaterealestate/views/object/view.html.php

```
<?php
// No direct access to this file
defined('_JEXEC') or die;
JHtml::_('behavior.tooltip');
?>
<form    action="<?php    echo    JRoute::_('index.php?
option=com_cocoaterealestate&layout=edit&id='.(int) $this->item->id); ?>"
  method="post" name="adminForm" id="object-form">
  <fieldset class="adminform">
      <legend><?php echo JText::_('COM_COCOATEREALESTATE_OBJECT_DETAILS'); ?
></legend>
    <ul class="adminformlist">
      <?php foreach($this->form->getFieldset() as $field): ?>
        <li><?php echo $field->label;echo $field->input;?></li>
      <?php endforeach; ?>
    </ul>
  </fieldset>
  <div>
    <input type="hidden" name="task" value="object.edit" />
      <?php echo JHtml::_('form.token'); ?>
  </div>
</form>
```

Listing 25: /administrator/component/com_cocoaterealestate/views/object/tmpl/edit.php

Chapter 6

The Cool Stuff

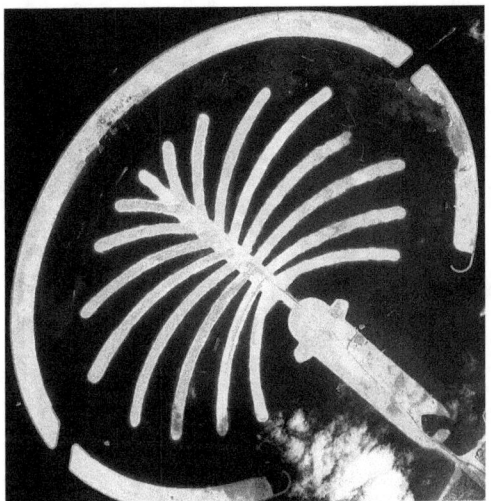

Photo: http://www.flickr.com/photos/lexgs40099/56656498/ CC-BY-2.0

Congrats!

The component exists and it was a challenge to build it. It is far from "ready to use" but I think you have now a clearer image of the structure behind a component.

At this stage, it would be good to think, for example, about using an IDE. I wrote the last chapter using Textwrangler as editor and I got lost in all these files. In the meantime, I installed Eclipse :)

WHAT IS MISSING IN OUR COMPONENT?

Well, that depends on your needs.

From a Joomla! perspective, everything is possible. From a client's perspective, you usually have to keep in mind that there is a limited budget!

But let's have a short list of missing features (feel free to add more in a comment[31]).

- **Managing the Portfolio in the Backend**
  When we have hundreds of listings, how do we manage them?

---

[31] http://cocoate.com/node/10216

- **Permissions**
  Who can add, edit and delete house listings?

- **Validation**
  If so many people are working on our platform, we have to validate their input to avoid failures.

- **Image Upload**
  How to upload the images in a convenient way?

- **Search**
  We need a possibility to search for houses.

- **Categories**
  Joomla! offers nested categories in Core.
  Let's use them to categorise our house listings!

- **Component Settings**
  What are the common settings for the component, e.g. the currency of the prices?

- **Updates**
  Joomla! provides an Update mechanism for your extension.

- **Going Big**
  Do we have more than one sales agent? If so, we need an additional "agent" table and a relationship between the objects and the agents.

- **Going Mobile**
  How to bring the house listing to the customer's mobile device?

- **Going Social**
  How to post the house listing to social media?

- **Working Together**
  Should we start a real estate community :)?

I stop here because this list will get endless.

THE FUTURE OF COCOATE REAL ESTATE

Maybe I am wrong but I think, for a beginner, you have seen enough to start on your own component development.

Now you can decide whether you want to try it or not. Have a look at my proposed tutorials in chapter Write your own Component.

THE DEAL

Let's make a deal between you and me!

I try to implement some of the tasks above, and when I finished a task I will write an additional chapter about it.

You try to implement tasks as well, maybe a totally different task, and contribute it to the Cocoate Real Estate version on GitHub[32].
I hope that it will grow and become the best Real Estate component in the Joomlaverse :)

---

[32] https://github.com/hagengraf/com_cocoaterealestate

Chapter 7

Write Your Own Module

written by Andrea Tarr - tarrconsulting.com

Photo: http://www.flickr.com/photos/45131642@N00/5987288907/ CC-BY-2.0

Modules are the "sidebar" content and widgets. They often work off of existing content and databases. An example would be a Latest Articles module with a list of the most recently added articles. As you will see in this chapter, to get full advantage of Joomla you take advantage of the Joomla framework contained in the *libraries/joomla* folder. Joomla uses object oriented PHP so much of what you find in the *libraries/joomla* folder is files of classes. By including these in your programme you let Joomla do your heavy lifting for you.

Joomla programmes by convention. It assumes you will structure your programme and name your files and classes in a certain way. This is one area where you don't want to be too creative.

Backend modules are contained in the *administrator/modules* folder and frontend modules are in the *modules* folder. Within those folders, each module has its own folder which starts with *mod_*.

The example we'll be working through is a Contact List, which in this example will be used to display a list of branches. The code is in a file attachment at the end of this tutorial. This is what the module will look like on the frontend (*Figure 1*):

Branches

Oneonta

934 Meyer Drive

Oneonta, NY 45682

413-555-3535

Belchertown

15 No. Main Street

Belchertown, MA 01007

413-555-1313

Brattleboro

12 Flat Street

Brattleboro, VT 67291

413-555-9987

City Island

Suite A

938 Parley Street

City Island, NY 10464

413-555-3950

Figure 1: Module Displayed in the Frontend

In the backend you will be able to select the category and how many contacts to display (*Figure 2*). (The backend screenshot in this tutorial is using the Hathor administrative template.)

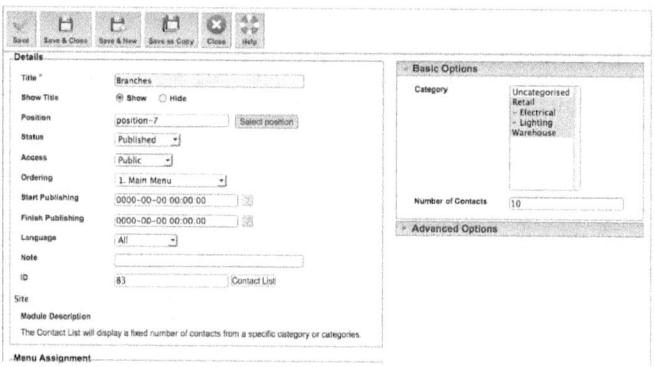

Figure 2: Module Options on the Backend

There are six main files, some in subfolders, in the *module/mod_contact_list* folder. In addition to these files, each folder should contain a dummy *index.html* file[33].

---

[33] Download the example module from http://cocoate.com/jdev/module

Path	File	Purpose
modules/mod_contact_list	mod_contact_list.xml	Define the module and parameters
modules/mod_contact_list	mod_contact_list.php	Main processing file - the controller
modules/mod_contact_list	helper.php	Helper functions to get the data - the model
modules/mod_contact_list/tmpl	default.php	The HTML for displaying the module - the view
modules/mod_contact_list/language/en-GB	en-GB_mod_content_list.ini	English language file
modules/mod_contact_list/language/en-GB	en-GB_mod_content_list.sys.ini	English language file for system strings

MOD_CONTACT_LIST.XML

The mod_contact_list.xml file defines the module, what version of Joomla it runs on, the files it uses and the parameters to be used. This file is necessary for the module to be installed. This is the first part of the file, which gives the basic description of the module:

```
<?xml version="1.0" encoding="UTF-8"?>
<extension type="module" version="1.7" client="site" method="upgrade">
   <name>MOD_CONTACT_LIST</name>
   <author>Andrea Tarr</author>
      <creationDate>November 2011</creationDate>
      <copyright>Copyright (C) 2011 Tarr Consulting. All rights reserved.</
copyright>
      <license>GNU General Public License version 2 or later</license>
      <authorEmail>atarr@tarrconsulting.com</authorEmail>
      <authorUrl>www.tarrconsulting.com</authorUrl>
   <version>1.0</version>
   <description>MOD_CONTACT_LIST_XML_DESCRIPTION</description>
```

The *<extension>* tag defines the type as module, the minimum version of Joomla and whether this is a frontend module (0) or a backend module (1). The method *"upgrade"* indicates that if a module folder with the same name is found, it will be assumed to be an earlier version of the same program that can be updated. If you use "install", any duplicate folder will prevent installation. The *<name>* and *<description>* tags are using language strings that will be translated in the language file. The language files will be explained later in this tutorial.

The next part lists the files. During the installation, these are the files that will be copied. If you have extra files in the zip file you are installing, they will be ignored. If you list a file that is not in the zip file, the module will not install.

```
      <files>

         <filename>mod_contact_list.xml</filename>

               <filename module="mod_contact_list">mod_contact_list.php</
filename>

         <filename>index.html</filename>

         <filename>helper.php</filename>

         <folder>tmpl</folder>

         <folder>language</folder>

      </files>
```

The main calling file is signified with the module attribute. The *<folder>* tag will copy all the files and subfolders in that folder.

The next section defines the parameters that you see on the right column in the backend. This section is enclosed in a <config> tag. The group of parameters is in a *<fields>* tag with the name attribute of "params". Each of the sliders is defined with a separate *<fieldset>*. First are the Basic parameters, where we choose the category and number of articles:

```
<config>

    <fields name="params">
        <fieldset name="basic">
            <field
                name="catid"
                type="category"
                extension="com_contact"
                multiple="true"
                default=""
                size="10"
                label="JCATEGORY"
                description="MOD_CONTACT_LIST_FIELD_CATEGORY_DESC" >
            </field>

            <field
                name="count"
                type="text"
                default="5"
                label="MOD_CONTACT_LIST_FIELD_ITEMS_LABEL"
                description="MOD_CONTACT_LIST_FIELD_ITEMS_DESC" />

        </fieldset>
```

Each of the individual parameters are in a *<field>* tag. The name attribute is used to get the parameter in your programme. The type attribute defines what type of field this is. Each of the types are defined in the Joomla framework. Common types used are text, list, editor, text area, category, calendar, radio, checkbox, checkboxes, media, folder list, and file list (full list[34]). You can also create your own types[35]. The label and description attributes use a language string found in either the global language files or in the specified extension language files.

The following Advanced parameters are the stock parameters which you should put on all your modules unless you don't want users to have these standard capabilities. All except for the *moduleclass_sfx* will work automatically just by including this code. For the *moduleclass_sfx* to work you need to add *<?php echo $moduleclass_sfx; ?>* to the class tag in the HTML layout where you want to allow the user to define a special class.

---

[34] http://docs.joomla.org/Standard_form_field_types

[35] http://docs.joomla.org/Creating_a_custom_form_field_type

```
<fieldset
    name="advanced">

    <field
        name="layout"
        type="modulelayout"
        label="JFIELD_ALT_LAYOUT_LABEL"
        description="JFIELD_ALT_MODULE_LAYOUT_DESC" />

    <field
        name="moduleclass_sfx"
        type="text"
        label="COM_MODULES_FIELD_MODULECLASS_SFX_LABEL"

description="COM_MODULES_FIELD_MODULECLASS_SFX_DESC" />

    <field
        name="cache"
        type="list"
        default="1"
        label="COM_MODULES_FIELD_CACHING_LABEL"
        description="COM_MODULES_FIELD_CACHING_DESC">
        <option
            value="1">JGLOBAL_USE_GLOBAL</option>
        <option
                value="0">COM_MODULES_FIELD_VALUE_NOCACHING</
option>
    </field>

    <field
        name="cache_time"
        type="text"
        default="900"
        label="COM_MODULES_FIELD_CACHE_TIME_LABEL"
        description="COM_MODULES_FIELD_CACHE_TIME_DESC" />

    <field
        name="cachemode"
        type="hidden"
        default="itemid">
        <option
            value="itemid"></option>
```

```
            </field>

        </fieldset>
```

Finish off the file by closing the tags:

```
        </fields>
    </config>
</extension>
```

MOD_CONTACT_LIST.PHP

The mod_contact_list.php is the main processing file for your program. It works as the controller in a Model-View-Controller structure. In the same way that we separate content from presentation and behaviour by having separate files for HTML/CSS/JavaScript, we separate the control of the program the data (model) and the display (view). The file starts out by checking to see that the file is being called by Joomla and not directly:

```
<?php
/**
 * Contact List
 *
 */


// no direct access
defined('_JEXEC') or die;
```

All your php files should start with this code.

We will be putting our data retrieval code in the *helper.php* file, so we need to include that file. It contains a class definition, so we need to use the require_once. The *dirname(__FILE__)* brings in the path of the current file so it can be used as the path for the helper.php file. Remember that a class definition doesn't actually do anything at the time it is included.

```
// Include the class of the syndicate functions only once
require_once(dirname(__FILE__).'/helper.php');
```

Next we will get the data by doing a static call to the class defined in the *helper.php* file and putting the result into *$list*. The *$params* is an object that contains all the parameters defined in the xml file.

```
// Static call to the class
$list = modContactListHelper::getList($params);
```

The next line just does a bit of housekeeping. We will be using the module class suffix parameter in the layout to construct a class, so we want to do some sanitising first. By putting it here, we ensure that it is done even if a designer does a template override.

```
$moduleclass_sfx = htmlspecialchars($params->get('moduleclass_sfx'));
```

Finally, we call the framework module processor which will put everything together and pass back the HTML to be displayed based on the layout file (*tmpl/default.php*). Since this is done as an include, any variables are still in scope.

```
require(JModuleHelper::getLayoutPath('mod_contact_list'));
```

This is the end of the file. Do not include a closing *?>* tag. The practice in Joomla! is to skip all closing php tags because characters after the php tag, including some control characters, trigger sending HTML headers prematurely, which causes errors.

HELPER.PHP

We are using the helper.php file to retrieve the data. We start the php file in the standard manner:

```php
<?php
// no direct access
defined('_JEXEC') or die;
```

We want to list the contacts in the Joomla contact table in given categories. Since we are using a table from a component that is defined in the standard Joomla way, we can use existing model definitions in our program. To do that we include the part of the Joomla framework that processes component models and do a static call to include the models from the com_contact component.

jimport('joomla.application.component.model');

JModel::addIncludePath(JPATH_ADMINISTRATOR.'/components/com_contact/models', 'ContactModel');

Now it's time to define the class definition. This class has no properties and getList() is the only method:

```php
class modContactListHelper
{
    /**
     * Retrieves the list of contacts
     *
     * @param array $params An object containing the module parameters
     * @access public
     */
    public function getList($params)
    {
```

The function starts by getting the global information, which is retrieved by a static call to the Application. This is what replaces the old global $mainframe from earlier Joomla programming.

```php
        $app  = JFactory::getApplication();
```

Next we get the database connection:

```php
        $db          = JFactory::getDbo();
```

Now we need to create a model object from the contacts. We use a static call to *JModel* telling it the component (*Contacts*) and the class prefix (*ContactModel*). Processing the model sets states to remember what state the model is in (like what the filters are set to) . When you are creating a module, you usually don't want to affect any states that the main component is in, so the ignore_request tells it to not remember the state from this processing.

```php
        // Get an instance of the generic contact model
```

```
        $model  =  JModel::getInstance('Contacts',  'ContactModel',
array('ignore_request' => true));
```

Next we set the application parameters in the model:

```
        $appParams = JFactory::getApplication()->getParams();
        $model->setState('params', $appParams);
```

Then we set the filters based on the module parameters. The list.start is set to 0 to start at the beginning and we set the end based on the count parameter that we entered in the module parameters. The filter.published set to 1 says to only get published contacts. The list.select lists the fields to return.

```
        $model->setState('list.start', 0);
        $model->setState('list.limit', (int) $params->get('count', 5));


        $model->setState('filter.published', 1);


        $model->setState('list.select', 'a.id, a.name, a.catid' .
                ', a.address, a.suburb, a.postcode, a.state, a.telephone
' .
                ', a.published, a.access, a.ordering, a.language'.
                ', a.publish_up, a.publish_down');
```

The next filter is for the ACL to make sure that only contacts that are allowed to be seen are chosen for display.

```
        $access  =  !JComponentHelper::getParams('com_contact')-
>get('show_noauth');
        $authorised                                               =
JAccess::getAuthorisedViewLevels(JFactory::getUser()->get('id'));
        $model->setState('filter.access', $access);
```

Then we filter for the category based on the parameter that we entered in the module parameters. Note that this is an array since we allowed multiples when we defined the parameter in the xml file.

```
        $model->setState('filter.category_id', $params->get('catid',
array()));
```

The last filters are for the language and to set the order of the contacts in the list.

```
        $model->setState('filter.language',$app->getLanguageFilter());
        $model->setState('list.ordering', 'ordering');
        $model->setState('list.direction', 'ASC');
```

Finally, we call the getItems() method in the $model object. Since we are using the getItems() method from the contacts component we don't need to write it ourselves. We can just use the one that already exists. All we needed to do was define the state of the filters. Then we return the list we just retrieved and close out the function and class. Notice that again we don't include a closing php tag

```
        $items = $model->getItems();


        return $items;
```

```
        }
    }
```

TMPL/DEFAULT.PHP

Now all we need to do is write the HTML that will display the list of information we have gathered. By separating out the HTML and putting it into a layout file in the tmpl folder we allow designers to use template overrides to change the HTML as they need. This file starts out as the other php files have: with the check to be sure that only Joomla has called it.

```php
<?php
/**
 * Contact List Module Entry Point
 */


// no direct access
defined('_JEXEC') or die; ?>
```

Next we put the HTML to display the list. It's a good idea to enclose the whole thing in a *<div>* with a class to identify the module type so that designers (or you) can add styling just for this module. This is also a good place to add the module class suffix. Putting the php code immediately following the module type class gives designer the most options.

```html
<div class="contact_list<?php echo $moduleclass_sfx; ?>">
```

Finally, we create an unordered list and loop through $list to display each of the lines. We then close up the enclosing div to end the file.

```php
<ul>
<?php foreach ($list as $item) :?>
        <li><h4><?php echo htmlspecialchars($item->name); ?></h4>
        <p><?php echo nl2br(htmlspecialchars($item->address)); ?><br />
        <?php echo htmlspecialchars($item->suburb); ?>,
        <?php echo htmlspecialchars($item->state); ?>
        <?php echo htmlspecialchars($item->postcode); ?><br />
        <?php echo htmlspecialchars($item->telephone); ?></p></li>
<?php endforeach; ?>
</ul>
</div>
```

LANGUAGE/EN-GB/EN-GB_MOD_CONTACT_LIST.INI

This is the main language file for the module. You put the language keys in your programme in all caps with a prefix of *MOD_CONTACT_LIST*. Assign the language string to be used with an equal sign and double quotes around the string. This is a different structure from 1.5. This new structure, which is much faster, does not allow blanks in the language key. This is an ini file, so you don't use the jexec or die at the beginning.

```
; Note : All ini files need to be saved as UTF-8 - No BOM


MOD_CONTACT_LIST="Contact List"
```

```
MOD_CONTACT_LIST_FIELD_CATEGORY_DESC="Select  Contacts  from  a  specific
Category or Categories."

MOD_CONTACT_LIST_FIELD_ITEMS_DESC="The  number  of  Contacts  to  display
within this module"

MOD_CONTACT_LIST_FIELD_ITEMS_LABEL="Number of Contacts"

MOD_CONTACT_LIST_XML_DESCRIPTION="The  Contact  List  will  display  a  fixed
number of contacts from a specific category or categories."
```

LANGUAGE/EN-GB/EN-GB_MOD_CONTACT_LIST.SYS.INI

The last file is the sys.ini language file. This file is just used on the Install and Update screens in the backend and only needs these keys. Those two screens have to access many extensions each of which could have large language files. By including short *sys.ini* files for each extension, the performance is improved.

```
; Note : All ini files need to be saved as UTF-8 - No BOM


MOD_CONTACT_LIST="Contact List"

MOD_CONTACT_LIST_XML_DESCRIPTION="The  Contact  List  will  display  a  fixed
number of contacts from a specific category or categories."

MOD_CONTACT_LIST_LAYOUT_DEFAULT="Default"
```

INDEX.HTML

You should put an index.html file in the root and in each *folder/subfolder* in your module to prevent the public from being able to get a list of the files by entering a directory in the address bar. The file can be as simple as:

```
<!DOCTYPE html><title></title>
```

PACKAGING THE MODULE FOR INSTALLATION

Since we've already created the xml file, the only thing you need to do to create an installation package is to zip up the files and folders in the module folder. Be sure to just zip the folders and files in the *mod_contact_list* folder and not to include the top level mod_contact_list folder itself.

If your files are already in Joomla! site you can use the *Extensions -> Extension Manager -> Discover* to install the module instead. Click on the Discover Icon to look for extension files that aren't installed. When your module shows up, check mark the box next to it and click *Install*.

Chapter 8

Write Your Own Plugin

Photo: http://www.flickr.com/photos/39747297@N05/5229733647/ CC-BY-2.0

A plugin is a kind of Joomla! extension.

The plug-in becomes active when a predefined event occurs. An event could occur e.g. when the event on ContentPrepare happens. That means while Joomla! prepares the content to be displayed our plug-in adds something to the preparations. Think of the core plug-in page break. If the event is fired, the plug-in gets active. If it finds the pattern *<hr class="system-pagebreak" />* in the text, it will implement the page break.

Joomla! has eight plug-in types: authentication, content, editors-xtd, editors, extension, search, system and user. These are also the names of the sub directories where the plug-in files are located. For example, plug-ins with a type of authentication are located in the directory plugins/authentication. A plug-in has to be installed via the extension manager.

Joomla provides for every type of plug-in predefined events, e.g. the content events

• onAfterDisplay

• onAfterContentSave

• onAfterDisplayTitle

• onAfterDisplayContent

- onPrepareContent
- onBeforeDisplay
- onBeforeContentSave
- onBeforeDisplayContent
- onContentPrepareForm
- onContentPrepareData

You find all the existing events in the Joomla! plug-in documentation[36].

Every extension can define its own events and this allows other extensions to respond to their events and make extensions extensible (*Figure 1*).

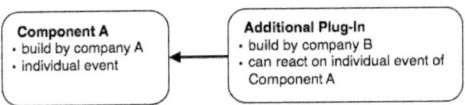

Figure 2: Plug-In, Component

EXAMPLE

To show a very easy example, we want to display a text string above the article text (*Figure 2*).

Joomla!

My special text

Congratulations! You have a Joomla! site! Joomla! makes it easy to build a website just the way you want it and keep it simple to update and maintain.

Joomla! is a flexible and powerful platform, whether you are building a small site for yourself or a huge site with hundreds of thousands of visitors. Joomla is open source, which means you can make it work just the way you want it to.

Beginners

My special text

If this is your first Joomla! site or your first web site, you have come to the right place. Joomla will help you get your website up and running quickly and easily.

Start off using your site by logging in using the administrator account you created when you installed Joomla!.

Upgraders

My special text

If you are an experienced Joomla! 1.5 user, this Joomla! site will seem very familiar. There are new templates and improved user interfaces, but most functionality is the same. The biggest changes are improved access control (ACL) and nested categories. This release of

Professionals

My special text

Joomla! 1.7 continues development of the Joomla Framework and CMS as a powerful and flexible way to bring your vision of the web to reality. With the administrator now fully MVC, the ability to control its look and the management of extensions is now complete.

Figure 2: Example Plug-In

---

[36] http://docs.joomla.org/Plugin

To implement our task we have to write a content plug-in that I called cocoateaddtext. We only need two files, the .xml file with the metadata (*Listing 1*) and a php file for our code (*Listing 2*)[37].

```php
<?php
defined('_JEXEC') or die;
jimport('joomla.plugin.plugin');


class plgContentCocoateAddText extends JPlugin
{
    public function onContentPrepare( $context, &$article, &$params,
$limitstart=0 )
    {
        $article->text = "<strong>My special text</strong>".$article->text ;
        return true;
    }
}
```

Listing 1: /plugins/content/cocoateaddtext/cocoateaddtext.php

```xml
<?xml version="1.0" encoding="utf-8"?>
<extension version="1.7" type="plugin" group="content">
    <name>PLG_CONTENT_COCOATEADDTEXT</name>
    <author>Hagen Graf</author>
    <creationDate>Dec 2011</creationDate>
    <copyright> :) </copyright>
        <license>GNU General Public License version 2 or later; see
LICENSE.txt</license>
    <authorEmail>info@cocoate.com</authorEmail>
    <authorUrl>www.cocoate.com</authorUrl>
    <version>1.0</version>
    <description>PLG_CONTENT_COCOATEADDTEXT_XML_DESCRIPTION</description>
    <files>
        <filename plugin="cocoateaddtext">cocoateaddtext.php</filename>
        <filename>index.html</filename>
    </files>
</extension>
```

Listing 2: /plugins/content/cocoateaddtext/cocoateaddtext.xml

After creating these files, you have to "*discover*" and install the plug-in - *Extensions -> Extension-Manager -> Discover (Figure 3)*

----

[37] Download the example plugin from http://cocoate.com/jdev/plugin

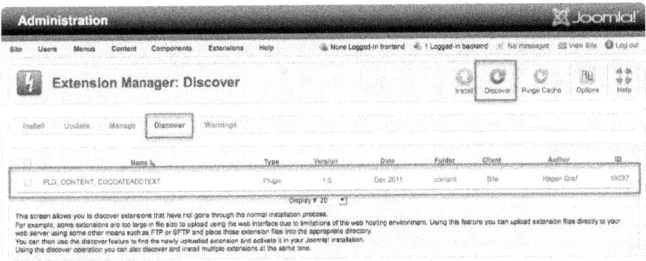

Figure 3: Discover and Install the Plug-in

After activating the plug-in manager, your frontpage articles will look like the ones in the screenshot in *Figure 2*.

Chapter 9

Write Your Own Template Overrides

Photo: http://www.flickr.com/photos/needoptic/5789554613 CC-BY-2.0

Imagine you are planning a Joomla! site with three different components. When you install the components they all come with predefined views to display their content. The views are created by the component developers and worst case is, that you have three different approaches to interface design on your site.

Of course, your client wants to have a unique template design and now you have to tweak the existing component views with additional CSS classes, different HTML tags or write a complete new markup.

You could change the code of the component. However, it is not good for your reputation because with the next component update, your changes would be gone!

This is the situation where template overrides enter the game.

Template overrides are basically a solution for the

> *Every time you hack core, God kills a kitten[38]*

---

[38] http://www.flickr.com/photos/hagengraf/2802915470/

problem. Even if there is no God available in your mind, and even if it's not core but component code, please, think of the kittens!

Let's assume you are a customer that uses our wonderful Cocoate Real Estate component.

Your idea of displaying the house listing is totally different from mine. Let's change it!

The component has a default template layout for each view. We want to change the frontend view, which is stored in the file */components/com_cocoaterealestate/views/object/tmpl/ default.php*. This file makes the page look the way it looks (*Figure 1*) and it is built around data which was collected in the file */components/com_cocoaterealestate/views/object/views.html.php*.

Figure 1: Default Object View

For our example we are using the *beez_20* template as a base. In reality you probably would start creating your own template but it would be too much at this point to describe the necessary steps so let's use the existing *beez_20*. Even if there is a Joomla! core update, your overridden files will not get lost.

Copy the file

/components/com_cocoaterealestate/views/object/tmpl/default.php

to

/templates/beez2/html/com_cocoaterealestate/object/default.php.

The template folder structure is like this:

- */templates* - the folder contains all templates
- */templates/beez_20* - the folder contains the beez2 template
- */templates/beez_20/html* - the folder contains the template overrides
- */templates/beez_20/html/com_cocoaterealestate* - the folder contains the template overrides for one component
- */templates/beez_20/html/com_cocoaterealestate/object* - the folder contains the template overrides for one view of the component

Uncomment or insert the last 5 lines of code (*Listing 1*).

```php
<?php
// No direct access to this file
defined('_JEXEC') or die;
?>
<h1><?php echo $this->item['title']; ?></h1>
<img src="<?php echo $this->item['image']; ?>">
<ul>
  <li>
  <?php echo $this->item['zip']; ?>
  <?php echo $this->item['city']; ?>,
  <?php echo $this->item['country']; ?>
  </li>
  <li>
  <strong><?php echo $this->item['price']; ?> €</strong>
  </li>
</ul>
<pre>
<?php
print_r($this->item);
?>
</pre>
```

Listing 1: /templates/beez_20/html/com_cocoaterealestate/object/default.php

The PHP function print_r() shows the content of the array *$this->item*. To make the output more readable I added tags between <pre> </pre>. When you reload your page you see now all the data. You can use the listing below for your individual template (*Figure 2*).

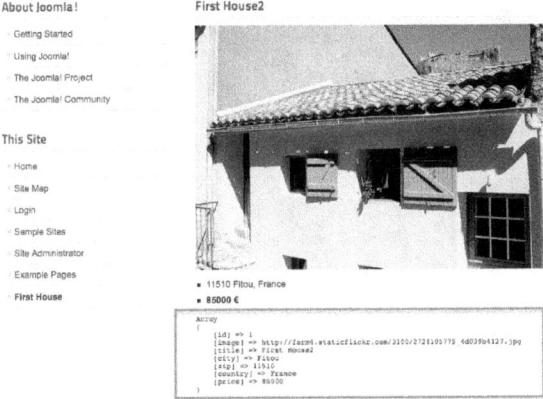

Figure 1: Overridden view Step 1

Yes, you should see the content of the array

```
Array
(
    [id] => 1
    [image] => http://farm4.staticflickr.com/3100/27241...
    [title] => First House
    [city] => Fitou
    [zip] => 11510
    [country] => France
    [price] => 85000
)
```

Depending on the component the array could be much bigger and more complex. In our case it is very simple.

Now you can pick the values you need and build your desired markup around.

Example: If you want to have the price in a *<div>* Tag with a special class it could look like this:

```
<div class="myprice>
<?php echo $this->item['price']; ?>
</div>
```

It is possible to use any kind of PHP statements in this file but it would be much better if the component developer offers all the necessary fields in the array so that you are able to concentrate on the markup.

MORE INFORMATION ON OVERRIDES

- http://docs.joomla.org/How_to_override_the_output_from_the_Joomla!_core
- http://docs.joomla.org/Understanding_Output_Overrides

Chapter 10

Write Your Own Layout

Alternative

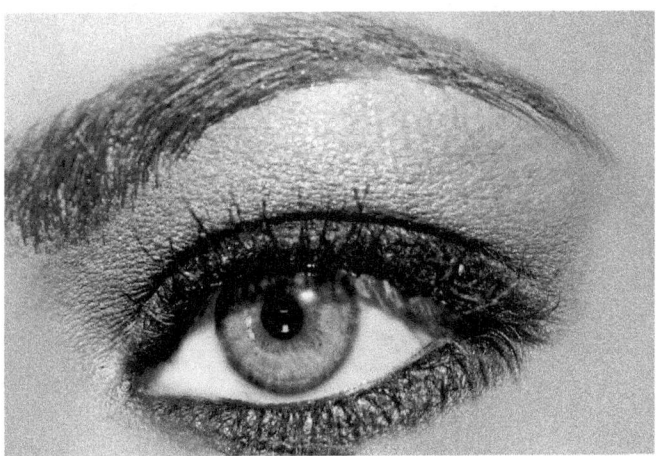

Photo: http://www.flickr.com/photos/pumpkincat210/4264425603/ CC-BY-2.0

Alternative layouts are a possibility for extension developers to avoid the necessity of creating template overrides and for template designer a chance to offer different layouts for existing modules and components.

Imagine, a component would come with three alternative layouts for an article. Sometimes it is a 'normal article', sometimes it should look like a product, and sometimes like a book page. Or a template would offer different layouts for the core login module. You only have to choose which layout you would like to use.

It is possible to create alternative layouts for

- components
- categories
- modules

The way of implementing the alternative layouts is exactly the same for components, modules and categories.

EXAMPLE FOR MODULE ALTERNATIVE LAYOUTS

You can provide one or more additional layouts to any module.

Depending on your needs you can place the layout directly in the modules view folder or in the template.

• If you are the developer of that module you should put the different layouts to the module view template (*Figure 1*). Afterwards you can choose the layout you want to display in the module options (*Figure 2*).

• If you are the developer/designer of a template you should put the different layouts to the template overrides folder html. There, you have to create a folder with the same name as the module and a subfolder for the view. It is the same folder that you use for template overrides. Obviously the file name has to be something other than default.php as this one has already been reserved for template overrides. And please do not use an underscore _ in the file name. For reasons I don't really know, it is sometimes not working. Afterwards, you can choose the alternative layout in the module option (Figure 3).

You can even translate the file name shown in the module options using the language files by adding the line

```
TPL_BEEZ_20_MOD_LOGIN_LAYOUT_MYBEEZLAYOUT="My Login Layout"
```

to the file */templates/beez_20/langauge/en-GB/en-GB.tpl_beez_20.sys.ini*, it will translate the file name "mybeezlayout.php" to "Alt Login Layout".

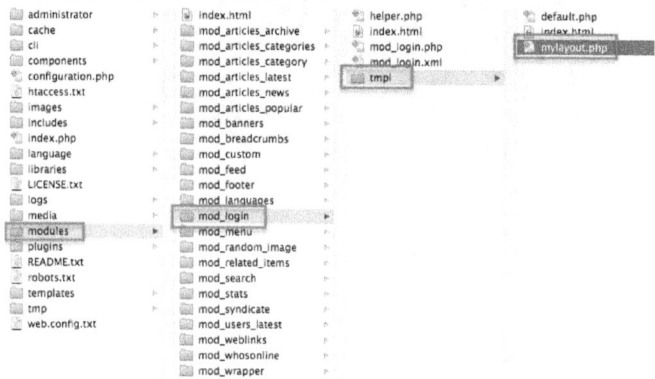

Figure 1: Alternative Layout in the Module Folder

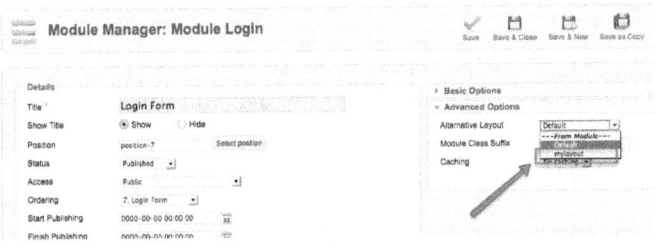

Figure 2: Alternative layout in module options

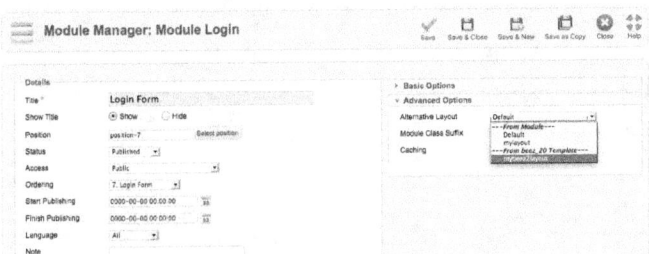

Figure 3: Alternative Layout for Module from beez_20 template

ALTERNATIVE MENU ITEMS

In addition to the alternative layout, menu item types can be added to the layout and the option items of that article can be controlled by defining them in an xml file with the same name as the alternative layout file. The presence of an XML file makes an alternative layout a menu item. For example, to create an alternative menu item called *"mylayout"* for an article you would create two files in the *templates/beez_20/html/com_content/article folder* called mylayout.php and *mylayout.xml*. If you wanted to include more layout files, you would add these files with underscores in the file names.

Menu item layouts take priority over component or category alternative layouts.

The XML file uses the same format as the core menu item XML files. This allows you not only to create a customised layout for this menu item, it also allows you to create customised parameters. For example, you could hide some parameters or add new parameters.

READ MORE:

http://docs.joomla.org/Layout_Overrides_in_Joomla_1.6

Chapter 11

Write Your Own App Using Joomla! Platform

Photo: http://www.flickr.com/photos/papalars/691515009/ CC-BY-2.0

The term Joomla! platform is quite new. It was introduced with the release of Joomla! 1.6 in January 2011.

HISTORY

Since the beginning of Mambo/Joomla!, there are files called *mambo.php* and *joomla.php* in the CMS package.

In Joomla! 1.0 these files contain 6,153 lines of code. These files also include a few other files and they were just "big". They were a reservoir for code which was used by core and third party extensions.

The files grew and grew, and over time it became jPlatform, a kind of operating system for Joomla!, and the CMS as a sort of application that runs on it.

Since Joomla! 1.6 the platform has been separated from the CMS.

The Joomla! platform is the framework on top of which the Joomla! CMS operates.

The idea of this separation was born after the launch of Joomla! 1.0 in the year 2005 and it took nearly six years to implement it. It will change the way developers, architects and service providers deal with Joomla! in the future.

Many companies and organisations have requirements that go beyond what is available in the basic Joomla! CMS package. Think of integrated e-commerce systems, complex business directories or reservation systems.

Let's have a closer look.

Numbering

What confuses me most when I heard of it for the first time was the numbering. But I found a very simple answer to that.

The numbering scheme for the platform consists of the year number followed by a sequence number, so 11.1 was the first release in 2011. The next release was 11.2.

The first release in 2012 will be numbered 12.1.

Release Cycle

Every three months a new version of the Joomla! platform will be released.

Package Content

The platform package consists of the files stored in the folder /libraries and /media and has no graphical user interface.

The platform source code is stored in the Git version control system GitHub.

code: https://github.com/joomla/joomla-platform

members: https://github.com/joomla/joomla-platform/network/members

Advantages and Benefits of the Separation

1. It allows developers to use the Joomla! Platform independently of the CMS.

   This means that you'll have the choice between different CMSs on top of the Joomla! platform in the future. This is really revolutionary! Joomla! is the only system in the world which provides that.

   There is still one core CMS provided by the Joomla! project but other projects like Molajo could use the Joomla! platform as a base, too.

2. It allows developers to contribute / add features more quickly.

   In the past it was very frustrating to experience that good code wasn't always included into Joomla! core. With the Joomla! platform stored on GitHub, it is very easy to fork it for your own purpose and it is easy, too, to integrate your code in the main branch.

3. 3-month release cycle.

   With this short release cycle it is possible to add features into the platform much quicker than into the CMS. This is useful for extension developers to add core features which are necessary for their extension.

4. It encourages recruitment of more developers, including larger corporations, who may have not, otherwise, contribute.

   This point is crucial and it will work when the responsible team for the platform starts embracing these new faces!

USING THE JOOMLA PLATFORM

First of all you have to download the platform.

You find the latest version on GitHub (https://github.com/joomla/joomla-platform).

- Manual: http://developer.joomla.org/manual/

- Coding Standards: http://developer.joomla.org/standards/

Afterwards you have to extract the file in your public web server directory (*htdocs*) and create a folder for your applications (*cli*).

In the folder */docs* you find the documentation and the coding standard of the platform. The files are in docbook format and it's a bit tricky to view them. Elkuku[39] provides a public filter for the documentation where you can download the docs as pdf[40].

Test Your Environment

The Joomla! platform provides no graphical user interface (GUI) in a browser like the Joomla! CMS so we have to use the command line interface (CLI) for our very first steps.

Depending on the operating system and the LAMP stack you are using it can be possible that PHP isn't installed correctly. You can check by entering the command php -version in your command line interface (Terminal in OSX[41], Command Prompt in Windows[42], Shell in all ..ix systems[43]. I am using OSX and MAMP and the result looks like this

```
web hagengraf$ php -version
PHP 5.3.6 with Suhosin-Patch (cli) (built: Sep  8 2011 19:34:00)
Copyright (c) 1997-2011 The PHP Group
Zend Engine v2.3.0, Copyright (c) 1998-2011 Zend Technologies
```

Hello World

To start simple we begin with the *"hello world"* example. Create a file hello.php and put it into */cli* (*Listing 1*).

```
<?php
define( '_JEXEC', 1 );
// Import of necessary class file
require_once ( '../libraries/import.php' );
// Load JCli class
jimport( 'joomla.application.cli' );
// Extend JCli class
class HelloWorld extends JCli
{
  // overwrite method
  public function execute( )
  {
```

[39] http://twitter.com/#!/elkuku

[40] http://elkuku.github.com/joomla-platform/

[41] http://en.wikipedia.org/wiki/Terminal_(Mac_OS_X)

[42] http://en.wikipedia.org/wiki/Command_Prompt

[43] http://en.wikipedia.org/wiki/Unix_shell

```
    // print something
    $this->out( 'Hello World' );
  }
}
// Call of the static method executed in the derived class
HelloWorld?
JCli::getInstance( 'HelloWorld' )->execute( );

?>
```

Listing 1: hello.php

Execute your shiny new app with the command php hello.php and the result will look like this

```
cli hagengraf$ php hello.php

Hello World

cli hagengraf$
```

Well, to be honest, I was happy when I saw the result for the first time but it didn't blow me away :).

Let's do another example

Your Last Tweets

Do you have a twitter account? Let's create an interactive app using the Joomla! platform and read the last tweets (*listing 2*)

```php
<?php
define('_JEXEC', 1);
require_once '../libraries/import.php';
jimport('joomla.application.cli');


class TwitterFeed extends JCli
{


  //Get Latest Tweet
  function latest_tweet( $username, $count = 5 )
  {
        $url = "http://twitter.com/statuses/user_timeline/$username.xml?
count=$count";
     $xml = simplexml_load_file( $url ) or die( "could not connect" );
     $text = '';
     foreach( $xml->status as $status )
     {
       $text .= $status->text . '

';
     }
```

```
    return $text;
  }

  public function execute()
  {
    $this->out( 'What is your twitter handle?' );
    $username = $this->in( );

    $this->out( 'How many tweets to view?' );
    $count = $this->in( );

    $tweet = $this->latest_tweet( $username, $count );
    $this->out( $tweet );
  }

  protected function fetchConfigurationData()
  {
    return array();
  }
}

JCli::getInstance('TwitterFeed')->execute();
```

Listing 2: twitter.php

When you launch the app with php twitter.php it will ask you for a twitter user name and how many tweets you want to see. Then it will display the tweets!

```
cli hagengraf$ php twitter.php
What is your twitter handle?
hagengraf
How many tweets to view?
5
Did you know? Member for 8 years 7 weeks :) http://t.co/L8tzB2kz
#drupal #wordpress

@brianronnow can you give me the wrong link, then I will update it

@brianronnow oh sorry :) the correct answer is 243 pages

@brianronnow the last update was 2 days before JDay Denmark
```

We are getting more advanced :)

The handling has still the feeling of being involved in a movie like War Games [44] from the eighties but hey, it uses twitter, asks for input and shows me tweets on a command line - wow!

A WEB APP

The difference between our first examples and an application which runs in a browser is the use of HTML code. If we print out the HTML code it can be rendered to a web page via a browser.

In our first web app we just want to show the base path of the application and the actual date. The output in the browser should be like this:

My Web Application
The current URL is http://localhost/jplatform/
The date is 2011-11-21 15:03:11

To try this out we need two files, an index.php file and an *application.php* file in the *includes* folder. If you want to create one web application based on one Joomla! platform you have to place the index.php in the root directory of the Joomla! platform and the application.php in a new folder called *includes*.

```
- build
- docs
- includes
-- application.php
- libraries
- media
- tests
index.php
```

The *index.php* consist of the following statements (*Listing 3*). Code is collected from different parts of the platform and in the end your app is launched with the statement command *$app->render();*.

```php
<?php

if (file_exists(dirname(__FILE__) . '/defines.php'))
{
    include_once dirname(__FILE__) . '/defines.php';
}

// Define some things. Doing it here instead of a file because this
// is a super simple application.
define('JPATH_BASE', dirname(__FILE__));
define('JPATH_PLATFORM', JPATH_BASE . '/libraries');
define('JPATH_MYWEBAPP',JPATH_BASE);

// Usually this will be in the framework.php file in the
// includes folder.
```

---

[44] http://en.wikipedia.org/wiki/WarGames

```php
require_once JPATH_PLATFORM.'/import.php';

// Now that you have it, use jimport to get the specific packages your
application needs.
jimport('joomla.environment.uri');
jimport('joomla.utilities.date');

//It's an application, so let's get the application helper.
jimport('joomla.application.helper');
$client = new stdClass;
$client->name = 'mywebapp';
$client->path = JPATH_MYWEBAPP;

JApplicationHelper::addClientInfo($client);

// Instantiate the application.
// We're setting session to false because we aren't using a database
// so there is no where to store it.
$config = Array ('session'=>false);

$app = JFactory::getApplication('mywebapp', $config);

// Render the application. This is just the name of a method you
// create in your application.php
$app->render();
?>
```

Listing 3: index.php

You find the code for the application in *listing 4*.

```php
<?php
// no direct access
defined('JPATH_PLATFORM') or die;
final class JMyWebApp extends JApplication
{
  /**
   * Display the application.
   */
  public function render()
  {
    echo '<h1>My Web Application</h1>';
    echo 'The current URL is '.JUri::current().'<br/>';
    echo 'The date is '. JFactory::getDate('now');
```

```
    }
  }
?>
```

Listing 4: /includes/application.php

If you are used to the Joomla! CMS you can use all bits and pieces you already know and build your own application.

I took the three examples from the Joomla! documentation page[45] and in the end I was impressed by the possibility of building something completely new based on the Joomla! code.

MULTIPLE WEB APPS

In our first example we installed exactly one web app (myapp) on one Joomla! platform. If that suits you, everything is fine. Imagine you have several apps you want to run on one Joomla! platform installation. For this purpose you need an additional bootstrap.php file (listing 5) and the following directory structure:

```
- build
- docs
- libraries
- media
- tests
- cli <- only if you have cli apps
- web <- the folder for the web apps
-- myapp <- the folder of one app
--- includes
---- application.php
--- index.php
-- anotherapp <- the folder of another app
--- includes
---- application.php
--- index.php
- bootstrap.php
```

The file *bootstrap.php* consists of one line of code and is necessary to show your web app the way to the Joomla! library folder.

```
<?php
require dirname(dirname(__FILE__)).'/jplatform/libraries/import.php';
```

Listing 5: bootstrap.php

MORE RESOURCES

There is a place on GitHub where examples are collected (https://github.com/joomla/joomla-platform-examples).

They are prepared in the multiple apps structure I described above.

---

[45] http://docs.joomla.org/How_to_create_a_stand-alone_application_using_the_Joomla!_Platform

You can download, extract and execute the examples in your Joomla! platform folder.

Chapter 12

Common Mistakes

Photo: http://www.flickr.com/photos/mike9alive/3630395512 CC-BY-2.0

Starting to develop software is hard. There are so many concepts, ideas, best practices, frameworks and dependencies.

You are usually so happy when your programme simply works. One code statement isn't that complicated. And the "Hello World" example always works well, but when you try to solve "real" problems, you are often lost and after a while you start trying everything to get it to work.

It was the same for me when I wrote this book.

I had so many situations where I didn't know "What is the correct way!".

And often there is no "correct way". People answered my questions concerning coding often with

> *Well, it depends on ... You can do it like this or like that, but be careful, there can be side effects ...*

November 13th, I saw this tweet[46] from Radek Suski:

---

[46] http://twitter.com/#!/RadekSu/status/135740923949756416

If I see this: http://wklej.org/id/624970/ I think we really need some kind of certification authority for Joomla! developers. #Fail

I asked him whether we could write a chapter on that topic and two weeks later I got his list of common mistakes.

RADEK SUSKI'S LIST OF COMMON MISTAKES

Getting Data from Request

Most common mistake make by novice Joomla! programmers is the method of how they're getting variables from the HTTP Request:

```
$id = $_REQUEST[ 'id' ];
```

That way, besides the fact that it's not validated, it also isn't determined from what kind of request exactly the data has been taken.

If you are developing a new Joomla! extension you should be certain which way the data is being delivered. For example, if these data are being sent from a form, it's most probable, that these data have been sent via the POST method.

In this case, it would be more appropriated this way:

```
$id = $_POST[ 'id' ];
```

However, this variable still isn't validated. Fortunately, the Joomla! framework provides an input class used to manage retrieving data from the HTTP request.

```
$jInput = JFactory::getApplication()->input;
// From GET
$id = $jInput->get->get( 'id', 0, 'INT' );
// From POST
$id = $jInput->post->get( 'id', 0, 'INT');
```

As you can see these data are also being validated as an integer variable.

There are also more validation filters available. For more information please visit: http://docs.joomla.org/JInput_Background_for_Joomla_Platform

Connecting to the Database

If you need to connect to the database you may have used a method like this:

```
$dbConn = mysql_connect( 'address', 'login', 'password' );
$db = mysql_select_db( 'table', $dbConn );
$query = "SELECT `data` FROM `jos_my_table` WHERE `name`='{$myName}'";
$results = mysql_query( $query );
```

First of, all it will not work like this in Joomla! because you don't know the database name nor the credentials for the db connection. And you don't really have to.

Here is how it works in Joomla!

```
// get database object
$db = JFactory::getDbo();
// get new query
$query = $db->getQuery( true );
// what to select
$query->select( 'data' );
```

```
// from which table
// do not use fixed db prefix - the #__ will be replaced with the right
one
$query->from( '#__my_table' );
// what is the condition
// do not forget to escape any variable you're passing to the SQL-Query
$query->where( 'name=' . $db->escape( $myName ) );
// set the query
$db->setQuery( $query );
// and load result
$results = $db->loadResult();
```

For more information please visit: http://docs.joomla.org/JDatabase

Files Operations

Because Joomla! has implemented an FTP-Layer to avoid possible problems on not properly configured servers, it is not recommended to read, and especially to write into a file directly using the native PHP functions. Also, file operations, like creating a new file, copying it, creating a new directory, should be implemented through Joomla! core methods.

So instead of:

```
$content = "My content";
file_put_contents( $content, 'my_file.txt' );
mkdir( 'new_folder' );
copy( 'my_file.txt', 'new_folder/my_file.txt' );
```

Use:

```
jimport( 'joomla.filesystem.file' );
jimport( 'joomla.filesystem.folder' );
$content = "My content";
JFile::write( 'my_file.txt', $content );
JFolder::create( 'new_folder' );
JFile::copy( 'my_file.txt', 'new_folder/my_file.txt' );
```

Loading Styles and Scripts

If you would like to add JavaScript or CSS files or CSS declarations the method to do this in Joomla! is quite simple.

```
// get current document instance
$document = JFactory::getDocument();
// add CSS style declaration
$document->addStyleSheet( 'media/css/my_style.css' );
// add some CSS inline declaration
$document->addStyleDeclaration( 'div#myDiv { border-style: solid; }' );
// add script file
$document->addScript( 'media/js/my_script.js' );
// add inline script declaration
```

```
$document->addScriptDeclaration( 'function foo( id ) { alert( id ) }' );
```

For more information please visit: http://docs.joomla.org/Category;JDocument

Sending Emails

As Joomla! supports already different methods for email communication, it is not recommended to send emails directly using the **PHP** core functions.

This is the method you probably know:

```
$to = 'nobody@example.com';
$subject = 'the subject';
$message = 'Lorem ipsum dolor sit amet, consectetur adipiscing elit.';
$headers = 'From: webmaster@example.com' . "\r\n" .
        'Reply-To: webmaster@example.com' . "\r\n" .
        'X-Mailer: PHP/' . phpversion();
mail( $to, $subject, $message, $headers );
```

And here is how you should do this in Joomla!

```
$mailer = JFactory::getMailer();
$mailer->setSender( array( 'webmaster@example.com', 'John Doe' ) );
$mailer->addRecipient( 'nobody@example.com' );
$mailer->setSubject( 'the subject' );
$mailer->setBody( 'Lorem ipsum dolor sit amet, consectetur adipiscing
elit.' );
$mailer->Send();
```

In my opinion the Joomla! method is much more elegant. For more information please visit: http://docs.joomla.org/How_to_send_email_from_components

Handling User State Information

While developing a script, we sometimes need to store some user state information like, for example, selected ordering, chosen preferences, and so on. Normally, we tend to use HTTP cookies for storing such data. However, cookies are quite limited in its functionality and newest HTML5 techniques are not fully supported at the moment.

The Joomla! framework provides an excellent method for this problem. Besides that, the nice feature of this functionality is that we don't have to worry about the type of the data we want to store. So we can store a string, an array or even an object.

```
$app = JFactory::getApplication();
// store state data
$app->setUserState( 'my_id', $myVar );
// get stored data
$var = $app->getUserStateFromRequest( 'my_id', 'my_id_in_request', 0,
'int' );
```

Also, please note that the "getUserStateFromRequest" method will update the user state variable, if a HTTP request (GET or POST) contains the "my_id_in_request" index, so you basically don't even need to set the state manually.

For more information please visit: http://docs.joomla.org/How_to_use_user_state_variables

YOUR List of Common Mistakes

I would love to add more of these tips to the list. If you know one, please post it as a comment[47] or contact me[48].

---

[47] http://cocoate.com/jdev/common-mistakes

[48] http://cocoate.com/contact

Chapter 13

Publish Your Extension to the

Joomla! Extension Directory

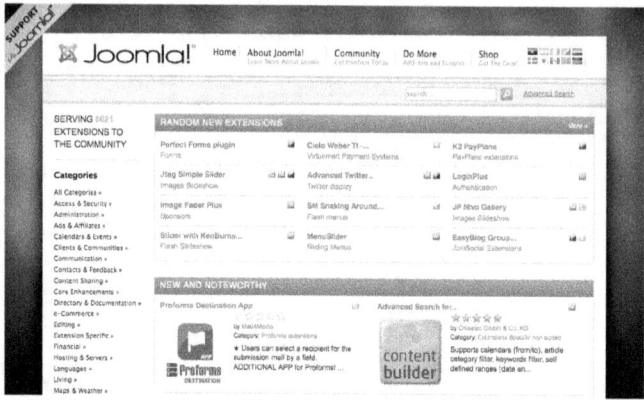

To offer your extension to millions of Joomla! users you can use the Joomla! extension directory (JED). The JED is the place where you find more than 8,000 extensions to enhance the possibilities of Joomla! core. After registering on the JED website, every user is allowed to submit an extension.

The directory is maintained by a team of volunteers[49]. The JED has its own area in the Joomla! forums called Extensions.Joomla.org - Feedback/Information[50].
The team also provides a ticket-based support for community members with listings in the JED. They are using a Joomla! help desk component[51] to manage the support tickets.

The directory itself is built using the Joomla! extension Mosets Tree[52]. It is structured by categories in three levels. The whole category tree is used as a menu on the site.

You can search the directory using the easy "one field search" or you can use the advanced search with the possibility to filter by various parameters (*Figure 1*).

---

[49] http://extensions.joomla.org/component/content/article/30

[50] http://forum.joomla.org/viewforum.php?f=262

[51] http://www.imaqma.com/joomla/helpdesk-component.html

[52] http://extensions.joomla.org/extensions/233/details

Figure 1: Advanced Search in the JED

Besides the search, you have a few charts and lists like

- New Extensions

- Recently Updated Extensions

- Most Favoured Extensions

- Editors' Picks

- Popular Extensions

- Most Rated Extensions

- Top Rated Extensions

- Most Reviewed

- Hot Extensions: An Extension will be shown as 'Hot' when it has an average of 150 views or more per day.

PUBLISH YOUR EXTENSION

To have an authentic chapter about the publishing experience, I did it by myself and tried to publish a module.

To publish your extension on the JED, you have to register on the site via the Joomla! way of registration or via Facebook login.

If you want to know all the details about the publishing process, it is probably best to have a cup of tea or coffee and read this document: Publishing to JED[53].

Where is the Submit Button?

---

[53] http://docs.joomla.org/Publishing_to_JED

You will not find a submit button or link on the frontpage. It is necessary to navigate to the appropriate category for your extension. In the category page you'll find the submit button.

The Submit Form

In the submit form you will be asked for:

- A description

- Links to your project homepage, the download URL, the demo URL, the documentation URL, a license page on your site, if you are submitting a commercial extension and a support forum URL

- The version, the license, the type of the extension

- The developer's name and email address

You have to add the zipped file of the extension and an image for the listing.

Hurry up with filling in the form fields, otherwise you get a message like this after submission

Your session has expired. Please log in again.

If everything went well, you see your freshly submitted extension in a pending state (Figure 2).

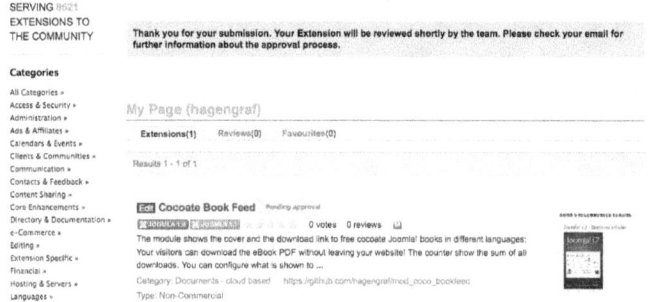

Figure 2: My Extension in Pending State

The Email Confirmation

After submitting you'll receive a nicely styled email with a lot of information. The most useful information for me was

What are some common errors that many developers miss and prevent publishing?

The most common errors are:

- Download link does not point to download/product page

- Domain or images use the Joomla Trademark and is not registered/approved

- Extension is commercial but has not included a link to the Terms or Conditions

- Developer attempts to restrict the usage of the extension in some way

- Security standards are not followed (index.html in all folders, usage of JEXEC commands)
- GPL Notices are missing in PHP/XML

And as it is written here I forgot the *index.html* in one folder :)

Edit Your Submission

After fixing my zip file with the additional index.html I was looking whether it is possible to edit my submission and it is!

Behind the link *My Page* in the JED you find your submitted extension. If you click on the *pending approval* link, the submission form opens again and you can edit all the fields.

How Long Do I Have to Wait Now?

Well that is hard. In my case there was the following notice:

> *Your extension is currently in queue awaiting review and approval by JED editors.*
>
> *There are a total of 197 extensions to go through before we review your extension for approval.*
>
> *Your listing was submitted on 22 November 2011. Listing approval time may be up to 21 days. You may not contact the JED Team inquiring about your approval as all listings will show error codes when reviewed and not approved. If you have questions concerning error codes you receive, please enter a support ticket.*

...

Waiting

...

One month later

...

12/26/2011 6:51 pm I received an email from team@extensions.joomla.org

```
Your new Listing named "Cocoate Book Feed" has been approved!
```

Download and install it immediately :) [54]

---

[54] http://extensions.joomla.org/extensions/social-web/social-display/external-widgets/19117

Chapter 14

What Is Git?

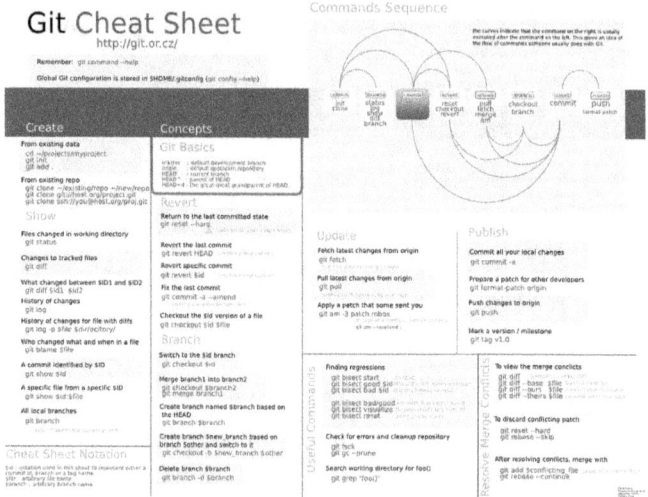

If you try to develop software with more than one developer involved, you run immediately into problems. While working, developers change something and all the other developers involved in that project need to update it in some way. If the changes were not that good, there should also be a possibility to rollback to a previous state or to restore the code in other ways. The problems even get harder when the developers are spread in different time zones all over the world.

CENTRALISED REPOSITORY

The first solution to that problem was a centralised repository. This repository was managed by a revision/version control system. Changes are usually identified by a number and are called revisions. For example, an initial set of files is revision 1. When the first change is made, the resulting set is revision 2, and so on. Each revision is associated with a timestamp and the person making the change. Revisions can be compared, restored, and with some types of files, merged (*Figure 1*).

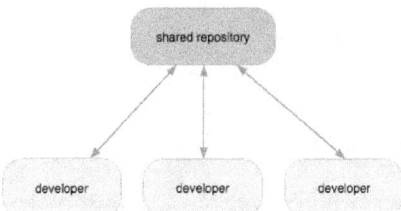

Figure 1: Centralised Workflow (Image htttps://github.com/schacon/whygitisbetter)

COMMIT

There are different strategies to work with different versions of code. One important word in this context is *commit*. Commits are operations which tell the revision control system you want to make a group of changes you have been making final and available to all users. Depending on the strategy of the system, commits are "atomic" or "file based". There are pros and cons for each strategy.

MERGE

If you have a big team of developers it is often the case that they are working on the same source code file. After a commit, the old and the new file have to be merged. This is easily possible in text files and nearly impossible in media files (images, sound, video).

VERSIONS

Most projects have different versions of the software like a stable branch and a development branch. Therefore, it is necessary to have a kind of tagging feature in the system.

DISTRIBUTED REVISION CONTROL

The repository is still central (the blessed repository), but in a distributed model the developer is allowed to have different versions/branches on the local workstation. The developer can decide whether the branches are public or local. This feature has a few advantages.

It is possible to

- create a branch, try out an idea, play around with it (commit, switch back), then merge it to the central repository.
- have branches from different states of the software

DECENTRALISED WORKFLOW

Depending on the size of the project, there has to be one person (*integration manager*) that pulls the changes of the developers in to the central repository (*Figure 2*).

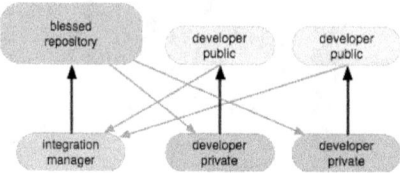

Figure 2: Decentralised Workflow (Image https://github.com/schacon/whygitisbetter)

DICTATOR AND LIEUTENANTS WORKFLOW

If the project is bigger, like it's the case for Joomla!, another level of hierarchy is used. The first integrators (*lieutenants*) are running a subsystem to merge in all the changes. Afterwards the next integrator (*the boss or the dictator*), which is only able to merge the changes of the subsystem, is responsible for the central repository (*Figure 3*).

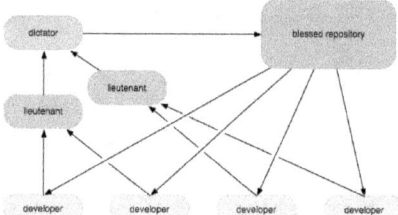

Figure 3: Dictator and Lieutenants Workflow (Image https://github.com/schacon/
whygitisbetter)

Software like GIT is called distributed revision control system (DRCS). Distributed version control or decentralised version control (DVCS) keeps track of software revisions and allows many developers to work on a given project without necessarily being connected to a common network.

THE NAME AND THE HISTORY

Git was initially designed and developed by Linus Torvalds for Linux kernel development. The name git is British English slang for a stupid or unpleasant person.

> *I'm an egotistical bastard, and I name all my projects after myself. First Linux, now git.*

GITHUB

GitHub is a web-based hosting service for the Git revision control system. GitHub offers both commercial plans and free accounts for open source projects. GitHub is a kind of Facebook or Google+ for developers, you will love it.

JOOMLA! AND GITHUB

In 2011, the Joomla! CMS and the Joomla Platform moved to GitHub - https://github.com/joomla

HOW TO START?

Just create a user on GitHub and download the GitHub client to manage your local branches. In your local GitHub client you have to sign in and can start creating repositories. Try it - it's easy and fun (*Figure 4*)

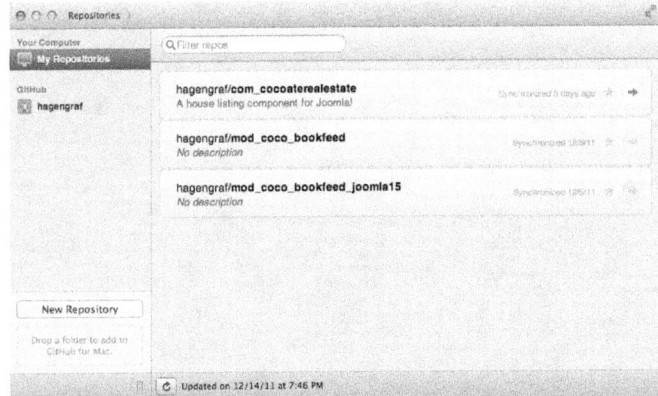

Figure 4: Git Client (OSX)

MORE TO READ ABOUT GIT

- Joomla! Documentation: Working with Git and GitHub[55]
- My first Pull Request[56]
- Why Git is Better than X[57]
- Pro Git[58]

---

[55] http://docs.joomla.org/Working_with_git_and_github

[56] http://docs.joomla.org/Working_with_git_and_github/My_first_pull_request

[57] http://whygitisbetterthanx.com/

[58] http://progit.org/book/

Joomla! Development - A Beginner's Guide

Chapter 15

Contribute Code to the Project

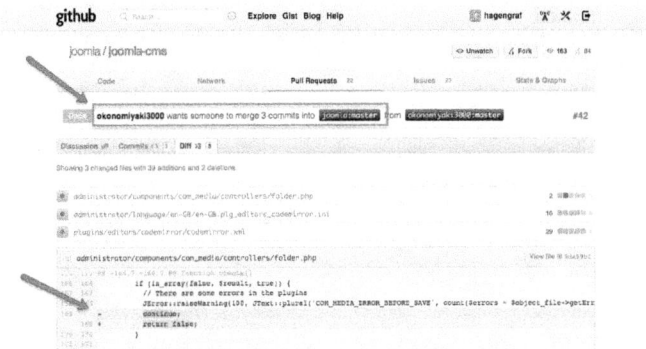

Someone has to write the code for Joomla! But how to contribute?

First of all, the code of the CMS and the Platform is stored here https://github.com/joomla

The Joomla! project runs a developer site with a focus on providing information and road maps to all the resources available for developers interesting in extending the Joomla! CMS, writing applications for the Joomla! Platform or helping to improve the Joomla! codebase - http://developer.joomla.org/.

After searching and reading, I realised that a newbie like you (and me too) is simply lost :)

MY FINDINGS

For me it was hard to find my way into contributions and it seems that there is no clear defined way how to contribute code. Maybe there is one, but I didn't find it :(I asked a few people[59] and I got various answers, so I decided to write up my experiences. First of all, I wanted to understand the structure behind the project. So let's try to figure that out. When you read the chapter things can be different. I wrote it in Dec. 13-16th, 2011.

JOOMLA! LEADERSHIP

The Joomla! Leadership Team[60] is made up of the leaders of the Joomla! Production and the Joomla! Community Workgroups. In case of code contribution we want to have a closer look at the Production Workgroup.

Production Working Group

---

[59] http://twitter.com/hagengraf/status/146907151917527040

[60] http://www.joomla.org/about-joomla/the-project/leadership-team.html

- **Task**: Create software that is free, secure and of high-quality—encompasses everything that goes into the final product, not just code but also documentation, internationalization and localisation efforts of all types.

- **Leaders**: Chris Davenport, Christophe Demko, Mark Dexter, Andrew Eddie, Louis Landry, Ian MacLennan, Sam Moffatt, Omar Ramos, Ron Severdia, Jean-Marie Simonet, Andrea Tarr

- **Responsibilities**: Core code development, patches, Joomla! Labs, Joomla! Bug Squad, localisation, internationalization, Joomla! Documentation, security, Google Summer of Code

- **Public Discussion Group**[61]

  Source[62]

Production Leadership Team (PLT)

The PLT is part of the Production Working Group[63]. Members are

- Christophe Demko
- Mark Dexter
- Sam Moffat
- Omar Ramos
- Ron Serverdia
- Andrea Tarr

The PLT itself consists of a development and a bug squad team.

I tried to figured out who are these people and how are processes organised.

I started to draw a kind of a map about that development team. It is of course not 100 % correct but this is how I understood it (*Figure 1*).

---

[61] http://groups.google.com/group/joomla-wg-production

[62] http://www.joomla.org/about-joomla/the-project/project-teams.html

[63] http://www.joomla.org/about-joomla/the-project/leadership-team.html

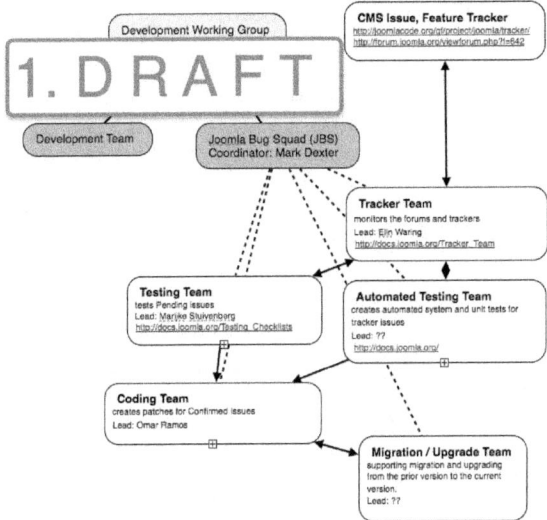

Figure 1: First Draft of the Structure

A very good overview over the current situation was given by Louis Landry at the Joomla! day in South Africa August 2011 [64]. Watch it - You will learn a lot!

Development Team

This team sometimes also is referred to as core-committers. Some of the members are also core-team members, but the term "core-committer" refers to team members who have full commit access to the Joomla! code base. The development work group aims at the development of a cutting edge, state of the art Web Content Management application framework. This workgroup is the driving force behind new versions, and building it. Along with the other working groups we try to realise this ambition (*Source[65]*).

Bug Squad Team

The Job of the Bug Squad Team is to identify and fix bugs in Joomla!.

I discovered a webinar recorded in June 2009 by Mark Dexter (Leader of the Development Bug Squad Group). It is a bit outdated in terms of Joomla! versions but I think it shows in a very nice way the idea of the Joomla! Bug Squad. For me it was a bit complicated to watch because it was in a "strange" format and I had to download and install additional software, so I

---

[64] http://vimeo.com/32799900

[65] http://docs.joomla.org/Development_Team

decided to convert it and put it on Vimeo[66]. You find the original recording on http://docs.joomla.org/Webinar:_Overview_of_Tracker_Process.

CONTRIBUTE CODE IN A TECHNICAL WAY

Nowadays Joomla! is stored on GitHub. You can fork the repository, browse through the code, change something and do a so called pull request.

You can see all the open requests at https://github.com/joomla/joomla-cms/pulls. Someone has to review and merge the requests to the core. You can even see the changes that are made in this pull request.

Example: okonomiyaki3000 wants someone to merge 3 commits into joomla:master from okonomiyaki3000:master (Figure 2)

Figure 2: Diff view of a Pull Request in GitHub

So now, anyone who is interested in that topic can comment and it is possible to have a public discussion. There is an app that collects all the pull requests against the Joomla! CMS and Platform and starts automated testing. At the end a member of the described infrastructure team above, has to decide and merge this request into the core - with one click of the merge button!

IT WAS NEVER EASIER TO CONTRIBUTE TO THE JOOMLA! PROJECT! TRY IT!

A good description of how you can make a pull request is documented here http://docs.joomla.org/Working_with_git_and_github/My_first_pull_request.

PROPOSE NEW FEATURES

It is absolutely necessary to talk about new features. The best way to do that is the mailing list. All posts are public and as an example here is a proposal for a new feature. You can read the

---

[66] http://vimeo.com/33649720

message and the discussion afterwards (A notification centre for Joomla![67]) (*Figure 3*) and you can even try it by yourself and potentially get involved on GitHub[68].

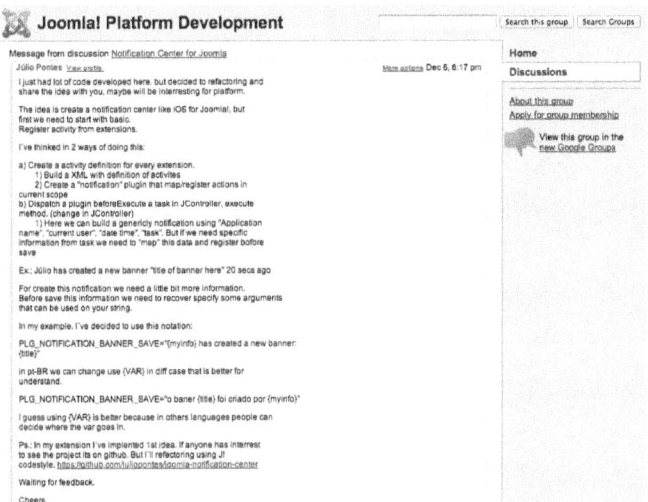

Figure 3: Proposal for a new feature in Joomla!

PLEASE COMMENT[69] IF YOU HAVE MORE LINKS, HINTS, IDEAS - I AM STILL LOOKING ...

MORE TO READ:

- http://docs.joomla.org/Development_Working_Group
- http://docs.joomla.org/Welcome_to_the_Bug_Squad
- http://docs.joomla.org/Bug_Squad
- http://docs.joomla.org/Bug_Squad_Checklist_For_Adding_New_Members
- http://docs.joomla.org/Bug_Tracking_Process
- http://docs.joomla.org/Patch_submission_guidelines
- http://docs.joomla.org/Learn_more_about_patch_files
- http://docs.joomla.org/Creating_a_patch

---

[67] http://groups.google.com/group/joomla-dev-platform/msg/0e0e5d39340f079f

[68] https://github.com/juliopontes/joomla-notification-center

[69] http://cocoate.com/jdev/contribute

Joomla! Development - A Beginner's Guide

Chapter 16

Localisation Using

OpenTranslators

Photo: http://www.flickr.com/photos/opentranslators

'OpenTranslators' is a new name in the Joomla! Universe. This chapter will explain the goal of this Joomla! Community Project and how Developers can make use of our expertise to improve the product they offer to the end users of Joomla! CMS & Platform.

As one of the biggest CMS projects, Joomla! is used by millions of users all over the world. Whilst the official language of the Joomla Project is English (British English *en-GB*), the users whose native language isn't English outnumber the English speaking users. Because of this, localisation (adapting a product to specific languages, cultures or groups of people) is very important.

Joomla itself is already being translated into many languages. This is done by the many hard-working volunteers in the different language teams[70]. Thanks to their efforts, the CMS is now available in many different languages.

---

[70] http://community.joomla.org/translations.html

For many of the extension Developers, however, the situation is different. It can be a big challenge for them to get their extensions translated. The smaller extension Developers can sometimes experience problems with finding Translators and managing their translations. To help our extension Developers, whose work we appreciate a lot, the OpenTranslators project has been started. We are here to help you increase the usability of your product, by bringing translators and developers together. We do this because the value of an extension translation shouldn't be underestimated. Both the Developer and the Community will benefit from such a translation.

In this chapter, we are going to share with you how OpenTranslators can help you, as a Developer. This chapter will explain how OpenTranslators works, what tools we use, why we believe that localisation is important and how both Developers and Translators will benefit from collaborating with us - and each other.

I18N & L10N - WHY THEY MATTER TO JOOMLA EXTENSION DEVELOPERS

As a Developer your focus obviously is on creating the code that turns your brilliant idea into a functional extension to be used in Joomla! CMS.

While creating this unique extension of yours, it may not even have come into consideration that, beyond the feature set you wish to share with the world, not all users of the many world languages share your preferred native language.

You could be a native English speaker and just haven´t considered that your potential audience might not read a single word of English. These potential users or customers, you will then never get in contact with.

But there is a solution to that, and it is right there at your fingertips. Make use of the built in internationalisation (i18n[71]) features of Joomla, the so called JText classes of the Joomla

---

[71] http://en.wikipedia.org/wiki/I18n

framework. With little effort you can ensure your extension has full i18n support and is prepared for localisation (L10n[72]). In return, Translators of any language can now share back their translations easily, without having to know PHP code, focussing solely on their main skill, which is translating. These combined will widen your reach and make your extension truly available to all potential users.

How to use the JText in your extension is explained in Chapter *Step 2 - Database, Backend, Languages, Listing 5*

i18n explained in the Joomla context

Since the release of Joomla 1.5, Joomla has had full support for i18n. This was done by choosing UTF-8 as standard, which enabled support for extended character sets. This means that Joomla core now can be fully translated and localised into any language, from the standard en-GB British source language set.

Considerations and what to look out for when making your extension i18n aware:

- Any string of text that are presented to the user, has to be translatable (ie: no hard coded strings)

- Think 'multilingual' when designing the visual of your extension user interface. Ask yourself if this short word in English might have corresponding words of more characters in other languages

- Remember that many users have a LTR (Left To Right) preference, while you are possibly designing in RTL (Right To Left)

L10n explained in the Joomla context:

A part of making your extension fully i18n aware is also to remember to have L10n in mind. Localisation has a great effect on how users experience your extension. There are local and cultural aspects to consider. Localisation is the part where you allow the Translator, the integrator or the end user to make your extension fully adapt to these local needs.

- Considerations and what to look out for when making your extension L10n aware:

- Ensure that local 'specials' like currency are adjustable and part of the i18n. Hard coded values could end up making your extension useless in parts of the world

- Make any text in images translateable. For example you could have image indicators showing 'New' or 'Updated' provided as part of your extension design. If possible make these into text so that it can be translated rather than the user having to replace them with their own images - or at least make the images selectable, instead of hard coded

- Think colours and their different meaning across the world. Various colours signal different things in different parts of the world. Let it be easy to localise visuals

Links and further reading about i18n and L10n:

- Joomla Documentation: Localisation[73]

- Colour Meanings by Culture[74]

---

[72] http://en.wikipedia.org/wiki/L10n

[73] http://docs.joomla.org/Localisation

[74] http://www.globalization-group.com/edge/resources/color-meanings-by-culture/

TRANSIFEX

Transifex is a turn-key solution to facilitate your product's translation, with the help of a wide community of translators and a great set of management tools. It is simple, fast and effective.

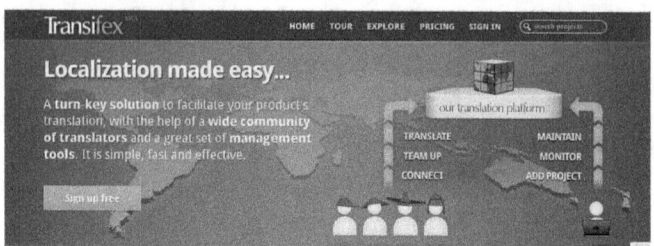

OPENTRANSLATORS

OpenTranslators is a Translation Project initiated by a multilingual volunteer team of Joomla! Community Members. We offer to work with our Joomla! Developers to 'give back' translations as a thank you for adding so much to Joomla! We aim to make these Joomla! extensions available in many languages by encouraging Translators of all experience levels to join our Translation Teams.

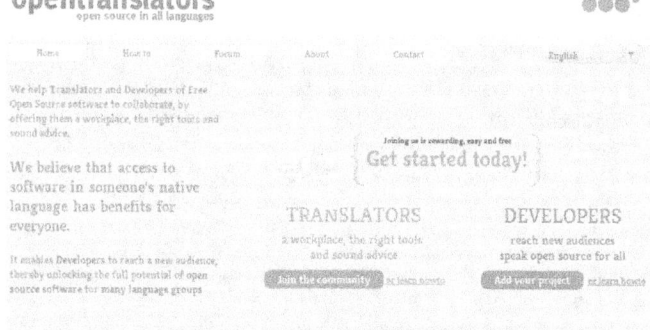

Well done. You have built your first Joomla extension. No doubt you are excited and want to share it with the Joomla world. But the user interface (the parameters etc) is written in English (en-GB) - those language .ini files need to be translated! This is where OpenTranslators can help you.

A little history

In the Joomla Project there is a very skilled group of Translators[75] who produce (currently 49[76]) localised translations of Joomla core. Until OpenTranslators began, each extension developer had to 'find' their own translators, usually from the users of that extension. This has worked particularly well for the larger, more popular extensions but has been difficult for the less publicised bulk of circa 8000 Joomla Extensions.

As more modern methods of translating have become available, enabling Translators to efficiently and easily work on or offline, a group of Joomla Community members identified this need and the OpenTranslators Project began end August 2011.

OpenTranslators chose to use Transifex, itself an Open Source Project being actively developed, as the platform for our translation hub. The core team of OpenTranslators, a team bringing Joomla development expertise added to extensive multi-lingual experience, joined with, and now are sponsored by, the Transifex Project and with a website, http://opentranslators.org , the task of growing the Translation Teams began.

The ultimate goal of OpenTranslators is to help create a vibrant, active and experienced Community of Translators who volunteer to translate Joomla related projects, who give suggestions and feedback to the Extension/Project Developers and who will encourage and mentor new Translators to join the OpenTranslators' initiative as well as the Joomla Core Translation Teams - all of which will help make Joomla and it's extensions available worldwide in many different languages.

> **Note:** *perhaps think of OpenTranslators as a 'dating agency'! We introduce Developers to Translators and vice versa. We do not control your project - that is your job - but we will offer advice and help if you need it.*

OpenTranslators Today - December 2011

OpenTranslators has created and maintains a growing pool of experienced volunteer Translators. All Extension Developers and Joomla related projects can tap into this pool simply by adding their project to Transifex without the need to manage hundreds of Translators individually.

With their understanding of the principle of a 'Volunteer Community of shared Translators', some of the most popular extensions for example redCOMPONENT (including redSHOP), NoNumber Extensions (including Advanced Module Manager) and StackIdeas (including EasyBlog) and many more (link to projects for translation) associated their translation projects and actively encouraged their existing Translators to join OpenTranslators. Together with the generosity of many volunteer Translators, the Translation Teams are growing both in the number of Translators and the diversity of language; bringing with them extended experience of technical translations and most with either developer or user experience of Joomla.

One of the great advantages of Transifex is that all translations can be done 'in the open' and, with the latest version of Transifex, Team Co-ordinators can nominate experienced Translators to proofread completed translations which will ensure quality translations are provided for your extension. Combined with Translation Memory[77], which offers Translators previous

---

[75] http://community.joomla.org/translations.html

[76] http://community.joomla.org/translations/joomla-16-translations.html

[77] http://en.wikipedia.org/wiki/Translation_memory

translations of strings, these translations will bring a consistency across all extension translations which was unachievable before.

Take a look at some of the OpenTranslators projects on Transifex, look at their resources, see what information they provide. Check out the translations and look at them from a Translator's view... and then learn how to add your own extension project so it truly can be shared with the world!

SETTING UP YOUR PROJECT WITH TRANSIFEX & OPENTRANSLATORS

Photo: http://www.flickr.com/photos/dannychoo/5076700146 (CC BY-SA 2.0)

In the previous paragraphs, we have introduced you to OpenTranslators and our vision on localisation and translations. We have also introduced you to Transifex - the platform we use to enable collaboration between you and the translators.

In this section we will focus on your tasks. We'll explain what you will need to do to set up your project, and what things you have to look out for while doing so. Keep in mind that our website has detailed manuals for developers - we're always working on improving them for your benefit.

This section will focus on the following areas:

1. Making contact with OpenTranslators

2. Working with the Transifex website

3. Setting up your project in Transifex

4. Using the Transifex client to maintain your translation files

5. Tips and tricks regarding Transifex, it's client, and translation files in general

We know you're busy and might be eager to get started, so let's carry on straight away!

Making contact with OpenTranslators

You can get in touch with OpenTranslators at any point during (or after) your setup. But in general, we recommend to get in touch with us before you get started. When you do, we can help you get started by pointing you in the right direction to make sure you make a good start! It is most important that you alert us at some point when you assign your project to use OpenTranslators.

You can contact OpenTranslators using Twitter @opentranslators[78], Google+[79], Facebook[80] or through our website[81].

Working with the Transifex site

As we mentioned before, we use the Transifex platform[82] to enable extension translations. Before you can get started with a project, you will need to register on Transifex. This is a simple process. Registering on Transifex is free - just like using Transifex is free for Open Source GPL licensed extensions.

> *Tip: If you don't already have a well known username, it is better to register with your real name or even better, both. We often use Twitter for communication so it is a good idea to add your Twitter username to your Transifex Profile.*

Setting up a project

Once you are registered on Transifex, you can set up your first project. We have described the steps on our website, in our developer 'how to'[83]. You can choose to use either the Basic or the Advanced method to set up your project - the outcome will be the same. When setting up the project, keep the following in mind:

- **Licence type:** When creating the project, you will be asked to choose the licence type for your project. Make sure to use "Other Open source" as your extension is licensed under (any version) of GPL

- **Access Control:** To assign your project(s) to the OpenTranslators' translator teams, you will need to set your Access Control to "Outsourced access" and select OpenTranslators

- **Tag your project:** Your project should be tagged with "OpenTranslators" without quotes. This will make it easier for our Translators to find your project and identify it as one that has been assigned to them. You can find this option under "Edit your project". You can see the list of projects currently tagged with OpenTranslators here[84]. You can also add your own name as tag here and any other tags you want

- **Use Bing or Google Translate for automated translations:** If you have an API key you can enable either one (or both) of the "automated translations" options. Enabling this

---

[78] https://twitter.com/opentranslators

[79] https://plus.google.com/b/103517388838387157233/

[80] http://www.facebook.com/OpenTranslators

[81] http://opentranslators.org

[82] https://www.transifex.net/

[83] http://opentranslators.org/en/how-to

[84] https://www.transifex.net/projects/tag/opentranslators/

option requires an API key. Translators can then use these tools to automatically translate strings for speed and accuracy where appropriate. More information[85]

- **Other Tools:** If you have two or more extensions, enable Translation Memory[86].

Using the Transifex client

The Transifex Client[87] is a command line tool that will allow you to easily and quickly manage your source files and the translations. This tool will be essential to you, as it will save you a lot of time when you use it. Using the client, you will be able to push translations to Transifex and pull translations to your desktop, svn or Github.

> **Note:** 'pushing' translations could be seen as uploading them, while 'pulling' them is similar to downloading them. You can also perform these actions manually on the site. A more detailed explanation can be found in the Client documentation.

If you need additional help on using the client, you can ask your question on our forum and one of your fellow developers will be able to help you out.

Making the translations ready for use in Joomla!

Of course, the goal of the translations is that you make them available to your users. You can choose to package the translation files in your extension package, or offer them separately as installable language packs. But before you are there, you might need to make some small changes to the files you download from Transifex.

The translation files Transifex outputs (for instance by using the pull function from the client discussed above), will probably need a little tweaking here and there to make them 100% suitable for Joomla. We have already documented some tips and posted them in our Tips and Tricks subforum. If you run into problems or have tips of your own, you can share them using the forum and we will make sure our experienced Developers will look at your post.

Links and further reading about your project on Transifex:

- Pseudo-translations for extension testing[88]
- Transifex 1.2 released December 2011[89]
- Webhooks[90]
- Transifex Glossary[91]

In this section, we have covered some of the tools at your disposal. However, we didn't mention one key element to make your translations happen - the volunteers who will be translating your extensions in their native language. The next part will explain how you can 'use' them and how Translators work.

---

[85] http://blog.transifex.net/2011/12/auto-translate-updates/

[86] http://help.transifex.net/intro/projects.html#translation-memory-exchange-tmx-files

[87] http://help.transifex.net/features/client/index.html

[88] http://help.transifex.net/intro/projects.html?#pseudo-translation-files

[89] http://help.transifex.net/server/releases/1.2.html

[90] http://help.transifex.net/intro/projects.html?#webhooks

[91] http://help.transifex.net/glossary.html#glossary

VOLUNTEER TRANSLATORS & YOU

How Developers can 'use' Translators through OpenTranslators on Transifex

All language teams are shared between all projects assigned to OpenTranslators. This means Developers will have access to continuously growing teams of Translators, all experienced in translating Joomla related products. This is especially beneficial for Developers who currently don't have a long-standing or well structured system, or any translation system at all. Developers new to translations will benefit from OpenTranslators' pool of Translators and might bring in some new Translators to increase this pool for others.

Developers who already have a system in place have nothing to lose in trying out OpenTranslators. Your already existing teams would join ours, in a true Open Source spirit, making collaboration and experience our strengths.

Our Translation Teams are available and accepting new Translators and ideas to improve our already efficient 'modus operandis'.

Getting feedback from Translators

Different language teams will opt for different strategies, for example:

- individual Translators can provide feedback by sending a private message through the Transifex messaging system
- Translators can provide feedback using the 'suggestions' tab when translating a string on Transifex
- posting on OpenTranslators' forum
- posting related articles
- sending tweets, either directly to the extension developer or via @OpenTranslators
- when our English (en) Proofreading Team is structured it will help non-native English speaking developers with their en-GB files

Interacting with Translators at the OpenTranslators' forum

Our OpenTranslators forum[92] is the perfect place for interaction between Translators, Co-ordinators and Developers. Each project or suite of projects is allocated its own forum and it is a place where everyone can and will benefit from everyone's input, feedback and collaboration, making it easier for newcomers to find and learn from the knowledge available to all.

Encouraging and motivating Translators by 'giving back'

To encourage Translators to maintain the translation of a project, most commercial extension Developers offer their Translators a copy of the product they're maintaining (limiting it to for example 1-3 freebies per language team)

Other ways to say 'thank you' and to encourage Translators are to:

• make sure you actually take and use the translations

• make a blog post or article on your website about the Translators who have contributed to the translation of your extensions

• send out a 'thank you' tweet, post on Facebook and Google+

• make sure you keep in touch with your translators by posting in OpenTranslators' forum or your own forum, especially regarding new releases/changes etc

• use one of OpenTranslators' banners[93] on your site

...but mostly just remember that the Translators are volunteers and that localisation is not possible without them

CONCLUSION

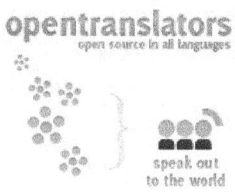

OpenTranslators is a project by and for Joomla! Community members, which brings together Translators and Developers. Localisation is our passion, and we'd like nothing more than to help Developers like you help themselves and their clients / community members by having your extensions translated in as many languages as possible.

If you are interested in tapping into our translation experience and our translator pool (currently over 260 translators in over 50 language teams) we welcome you to join us. Collaborating with OpenTranslators is free, simple and fun. If we've sparked your interest, we

---

[92] http://opentranslators.org/en/forum

[93] http://opentranslators.org/en/opentranslators-media-kit

recommend you check out our site, take a tour on Transifex, read our manuals or say "Hello" on our site, or the social media site of your choice. We look forward to hearing from you!

from your fellow Joomla! Community Members, the OpenTranslators Team.

Chapter 17

written by Alex Andrea

Running a Business Around

Joomla! Extensions

Photo: http://www.flickr.com/photos/73024773@N07/6589595017 (sourcecoast)

Over three years ago, I left a full-time job and decided to do Joomla! development full-time, starting SourceCoast[94] with a business partner. At first, we started doing custom client work: Joomla! installations, site setups, content insertion, site structure, etc. However, early on, we realised that we enjoyed the extension creation and support portion more than the client back-and-forth. What we didn't know was the best way to start turning extension development into a business.

In 2008 and 2009, we went to multiple Joomla-related events and attended every session we could on how to create a business around Joomla! extensions. While all the sessions were great,

---

[94] http://www.sourcecoast.com/

they all focused most on the GPL aspect of Joomla!, what its requirements were, and ways you could go about 'selling' your services. However, each discussion stopped right where the actual business setup, structure, how to manage extensions and users, and everything else I wanted to know should have been.

So, this chapter is our attempt to contribute back what we've learned initially by observing other developers and, eventually, by trial and error on our own. Hopefully, it will provide a general overview of the day-to-day tasks that we go through in the development, support, promotion, and continuing operations of SourceCoast.

THE 4 MAJOR ROLES OF AN EXTENSION BUSINESS

At SourceCoast, there are 4 major areas that we focus on: Product, Support, Business Model/ Pricing, and Promotion. This excludes some of the more mundane things, such as bookkeeping and accounting, but as we progressively manage to get each of those 4 areas executing better, our business has thrived.

1. PRODUCT

The most important thing when running an extension business is obviously having a good product. There are many ways to come up with ideas for extensions, but there are no guarantees that it will gain the traction needed to turn it into a full-blown business.

For us, our main product, JFBConnect (a Facebook integration tool for Joomla!) [95] was originally proposed by a client of ours. They wanted to add a Facebook Login button to their site to make logging in simpler for their users. We started development on the extension right away, and by the time we had the initial prototype, the client decided to go in a different direction. In an effort to make a little money back from our time investment, and because we thought it was a great idea in a non-filled market, we decided to start selling it. The extension was basic, but was a great starting point.

When starting out, first and foremost, you need to start small. Yes, it'd be great if you could make the 'next' shopping cart that handles all currencies, all shipping, and a slew of other things. However, it's unreasonable to assume you can do this when: you're still small, you're not making any money off of the new product yet, and you're not getting feedback yet from your users. If you shoot too big to start, you'll end up hurting yourself in the long run, if you even make it that far. You need early adopters that want a lower price and less features, so that you can go on to add more features, bug-squash, get more customers and eventually, even raise prices.

2. BUSINESS MODEL

Once you have an extension that you think has a market and is worth selling, the next, and possibly most difficult thing for developers, is actually starting a business around it. Pricing is the first step in this process, and there are a ton of different ideas on how to price something the best:

- Free "Community" version with paid support

- Free "Community" version with a supported 'pro' version

- Paid version only, with support

In all cases above, the paid version is on some 'subscription' period basis. Once you plan to include support for a payment, you **must** set a time limit on the duration. After that period is

---

[95] http://www.sourcecoast.com/jfbconnect/

over, since the extension is GPL, the user is free to continue using it. However, if they want support or need an upgrade (if not available as a free version), they'll need to re-subscribe. A duration based on a time period, a version number, or something similar is critical or else you could end up supporting some users forever. A 'lifetime' subscription sounds like a great selling point, but it will burn you in the long run.

At SourceCoast, we have a simple philosophy for our commercial extensions: We don't offer 'community', or free, versions. For us, offering a free version of your extension devalues the overall experience, and it causes a lot more problems than (ideally) it would solve. What we've seen and heard from other developers we've spoken with is that when they have a free version, it generally causes the following issues:

- **'xyz' is a necessity!** - Users have their own ideas of what should be in the free and pro versions. If you dictate something is pro-only, some users will be very upset that such a feature isn't included in their version.

- **Users don't read the feature list first** - If it's free, they'd rather just install and try it before understanding the features and limitations. This is a poor overall experience for the users, doesn't give your extension a fair shot, and may end up hurting you in reviews.

- **Extra time costs** - If you have a free and pro version, you're increasing your effort by developing, packaging, and testing both versions. That time could be better spent on one, better version.

- **It's harder to sell the upgrade** - When a user is going from free with 50 features, it's harder to sell them the extra 25 features. When they're paying for all 75 features, they feel like they're getting more (for the same price!)

- **Free can give the wrong experience** - If a user runs into issues with the free version, but there's no support, how can they trust that paying will solve their issue?

While there are some huge extensions out there that offer free versions, it's simply not how we could operate on our budget and on a team of only 2 developers. That's not to say our way is right for everyone, it's just what works for us.

Pricing

Now that you've decided on a model for your extensions, you actually need to determine the price. Again, from our experience, and contrary to what you might expect, there's one equation that we firmly believe in when it comes to pricing:

Higher Price == Happier Customers

It may sound crazy at first, but ideally, you can get the same amount of total money, from less users. While you may think you want tons of users, think of the benefits that you, and your customers, gain from a higher price and less users:

Lower overall support - For a small team, this gives you more time to focus on those users that need support. The support section details this more, but support will be *the* most critical aspect of your business.

More time to develop - Less support allows for more time for other things: documentation and development.

Users think before they buy! - Again, if your extension is free or promises the world for $5, users will buy without hesitation. If a user's experience isn't great, regardless of the price, they won't be happy.

Paying customers understand value - If you've ever read some reviews on the JED, they're wildly inconsistent. Some users bash free extensions. Others lump praise on overpriced extensions that under-deliver. When you price it correctly, you at least get the users that understand that free isn't always better. Those are the users you want. They'll understand that a bug-fix may take 2 days or that conflicts occur. Unreasonable users are not good customers. Unreasonable users a lot of the time only use free (or the cheapest) extensions. Let them use something else.

Of course, higher price doesn't mean an exorbitant price. Every market is different. Look at your competitors. Look at their features. Look at their price. When we started with JFBConnect, it was $15 for a minimal set of features. That was a 'high' price in a non-existent market at the time and for an extension that didn't do much, in all honesty. As features were added, we steadily increased the price from $15 to $20, $30, and are now at $50 for a 6-month subscription.

Refund Policy

When we first started out, we had the same feeling we hear from so many other developers: It's GPL, you can't give refunds or users will steal your stuff! Because of this, we, like many other extension clubs, had a strict no-refund policy. It made sense. It's GPL software. There are no license checks. There is no way to return the extension if a user gets a refund. How could we possibly allow for refunds? There are 2 great answers: Chargebacks and customer trust.

Chargebacks are the bane of any digital seller. When a user purchases a product through PayPal (or any other merchant), if they dispute those charges, you are responsible for proving you shipped the product or delivered something to them. Download logs and IP addresses almost never work as proof, and a no-return policy doesn't either, so what do you do? Nothing. And what happens? The merchant decides against you, refunds the money to the user and also hits you with a $20-$60 chargeback fee. This is a fee from the credit card companies for doing a dispute against the vendor.

Without a refund policy, this is the course of unhappy users. It not only nullifies their sale and leaves you with an unhappy customer, it ends up costing you extra money!

Users want to be assured that you have faith in your product and are willing to offer a refund if it doesn't fit their needs. Having a refund policy breaks down just about all barriers to the sale and builds that customer trust.

Our Results of a 30-Day Refund Policy

At the end of August 2010, we increased our rates by 60%, going from $30 to $50 on a 6-month subscription and $50 to $85 on a 1-year. At the same time, we instituted a 30-day money back guarantee. At that point, dollar volume of sales had been increasing about 20% month. In September, sales were up by 13%, and in the following months, they returned to a 15-25% monthly increase on average. The overall picture was that a 60% increase in pricing did not have a substantial impact on income. Additionally, it directly led to less customers, which from a support and development standpoint, was a great win for us.

It's impossible to say that our refund policy was the main reason the pricing increase didn't affect our overall revenue. Since then, however, SourceCoast has seen only one chargeback in the last year, whereas we would have received one or two a month previously, saving us about $20-50 in fees. Refunds have consistently stayed below 5% of sales, and generally are under 1% of total subscriptions every month. Even with those refunds, we've ensured that anyone who tries to use our extension is happy, which is great for good-will and publicity. If a user is unhappy, you want to ease them so they don't complain publicly about the extension or your business. Let them simply request a refund and go on their way.

3. SUPPORT

Far and away the most critical aspect of an extension is the support you provide for it. Even if your extension has all the bells and whistles possible, and even if it's extremely simple to use, users will run into issues. Server configurations, Joomla! settings, extension conflicts, you name it. Not all will be your extension's fault directly, but most users won't know that, won't understand it when you tell them, and most of all, won't care. They paid for your product - they, rightfully, will expect you to help resolve the problem however you can. It can't be overstated that your customers overall happiness will come from the support they receive. Without happy customers, you will receive poor reviews and lose out on essential word-of-mouth promotion, thus hurting your overall business.

There are multiple facets of support, and providing great support doesn't mean you have to be strapped to your computer all day answering questions (though you will need to be at times). To do support correctly, you need to be prepared for your users support needs beforehand, through documentation, and also at the time of need through "tech support".

Documentation

Very few, if any, people like writing documentation. When done right, having great documentation will make your users happier and save you an immense amount of time. Documentation is all-encompassing. Your extension itself should have clear descriptions of parameters and what each setting will do. There should be installation and configuration guides for every feature of your extension that users can skim through. There needs to be common support questions answering issues that you hear commonly from your users (server, configuration, conflict, styling, etc), or anticipated questions for a new release. Depending on your extension, there could possibly be 'advanced' guides for using some of the function calls or information on how to extend some of the functionality.

Above all, remember that documentation is an ongoing process. With each release, you should evaluate what information you have available and revise it where necessary.

Tech Support

Will your users read your documentation? For installation and configuration, probably. For support, probably not. When they come with questions, you need to be ready.

SourceCoast uses a forum-based technical support area, because it allows users to try to find their own answers. If you use a ticket-based system, questions and answers are hidden, which results in many repeated questions. Forums aren't perfect, and your method of tech support will depend on your needs.

Once you start getting tech support questions, the process should be simple. If your documentation is perfect, you'll be able to simply point them to their answer, instead of repeating the same answer for each user. If the answer isn't readily available, figure out the solution help that user. Then, determine if this is a question that may be asked again or has been asked before, and if so, document it for later reference.

If you've already written a detailed response, and it's fresh in your mind, that's the time to document it!

4. PROMOTION

Once you have an extension available, you need to get the word out about it. This can always be a daunting process, and there's no perfect way to do it. The main point of promotion isn't necessarily to make a sale immediately. It's to make sure your brand is known and that when a user needs to purchase from you, they already feel familiar with your company or brand. Promotion is a long term endeavour, and like everything else, needs to be refined with time. The following are just a few critical, yet free, ways to promote your products.

Joomla! Extension Directory

This is the most obvious, but can't be overstated. Being listed here doesn't guarantee success. However, without a JED listing, potential users will question why you're not listed, and may find other competitors that are. In addition, the reviews received here are moderated and a great way for prospective users to get an unbiased opinion before their purchase.

Blog

Use a blog to post about new updates, what you're working on, sites that started using your extension, or just about anything related to your products. Some users will subscribe to your feed to stay up-to-date. More importantly, you can submit your blog to Joomla! content aggregators like Joomla! Connect[96] and Joomla! Reader[97]. Each blog post can reach thousands of users, and each one of them is a potential customer!

Social Networking

Facebook, Twitter, etc. - you know the drill. Like your blog posts, tweet about updates. Use the LinkedIn Share button to post your content to professional network. Whatever social channels you have at your disposal, use them. They're free and they can hit a huge audience with just a little effort.

5. HARD WORK AND DISCIPLINE PAYS OFF

It's extremely generic to say, but hard work, dedication to your users, and constantly refining your process is the key to success. While everything above has worked for us, it's taken us years to get to this point. It's also possible that different choices along the way could have worked out better. Use the above as a guide for your own business, but don't feel it's etched in stone.

---

[96] http://connect.joomla.org/

[97] http://joomlareader.com/

Chapter 18

What Is PHP?

Photo: http://www.flickr.com/photos/myhsu/3040774379 CC-BV-2.0

PHP is a general-purpose server-side scripting language originally designed for web development to produce dynamic web pages. For this purpose, PHP code is embedded into the HTML source document and interpreted by a web server with a PHP processor module, which generates the web page document. It also has evolved to include a command-line interface capability and can be used in standalone graphical applications.

PHP was originally created by Rasmus Lerdorf in 1995. The main implementation of PHP is now produced by The PHP Group and serves as the de facto standard for PHP as there is no formal specification. PHP is free software released under the PHP License which is incompatible with the GNU General Public License due to restrictions on the usage of the term PHP.

While PHP originally stood for "Personal Home Page", it is now said to stand for "PHP: Hypertext Preprocessor", a recursive acronym[98].

The last stable version of PHP is **5.3.8** which was published in **August 2011**.

Joomla! is written in PHP. Thousands of files contain PHP code which was written over the last years. Joomla! consists of more than 500.000 lines of PHP code. It would need 244 person-years to develop it! (Joomla! estimated cost[99])

---

[98] http://en.wikipedia.org/wiki/Php

[99] http://www.ohloh.net/p/joomla/estimated_cost

When Joomla! was founded, the developers used mainly PHP 4.x which was very common these days. It was and partly is a challenge to rewrite the legacy code to use as many as possible features of PHP 5.x.

Let's have a short overview of PHP. If you ever had a programming course in school, you will remember most of the statements. If you are totally new, just have a look and try to understand the code. The example files are attached at the end of this page. It is a very good idea to try the examples on your own machine.

WHERE IS MY PHP?

If you use a LAMP bundle, PHP is inbuilt. Usually it is a binary file, tied to the Apache Web server as a module. When you start the Web server, PHP is ready to run. PHP has feature called phpInfo. It shows the configuration of everything which is related to your PHP interpreter. In MAMP, you can click on phpInfo to see that page (*Figure 1*).

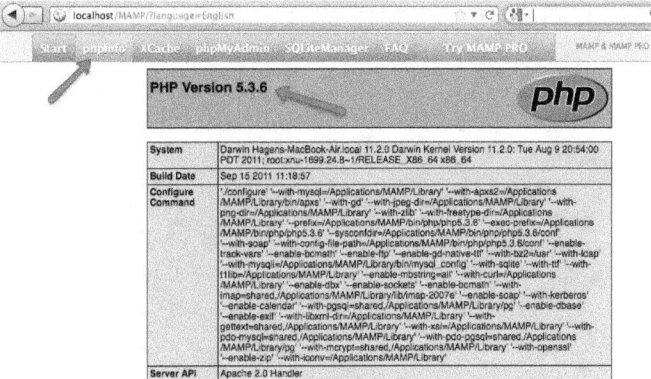

Figure 1: phpinfo via MAMP

It is very easy to produce the same output on your own. Just create an empty file with the name *phpinfo.php* (the name doesn't matter, could be also *joomlarocks.php*) in your editor and type in this code (*Listing 1*).

```php
<?php
phpinfo();
?>
```

Listing 1: phpinfo.php

Place the file in the */htdocs* folder access it via *http://localhost/* and click on the filename (*Figure 2*).

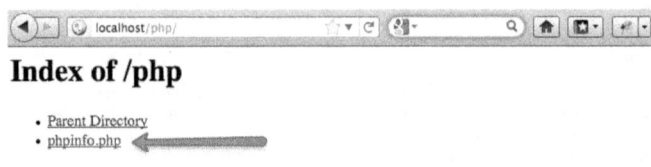

Index of /php

- Parent Directory
- phpinfo.php ◄━━━━━

Figure 2: Webserver Directory

Attention:

Depending on the the LAMP bundle you are using

- the domain localhost is tied to various ports. The default setting in MAMP e.g. is port 8888 and you have to write *http://localhost:8888*. Check your port in the documentation. If it is port 80 it is the default port of "the internet" and it is not necessary to write it. *http://localhost:80* is the same then *http://localhost*.

- you usually see a directory when accessing *http://localhost*. This is a configuration of your Apache web server. If you don't see a directory, create an additional folder in */htdocs* e.g. php and access it via *http://localhost/php*. If you still do not see a directory, access the file directly via *http://localhost/php/phpinfo.php* and search for a solution in the documentation of your LAMP bundle.

As you see, PHP programming starts very simple :) Any PHP script is built out of a series of statements.

HELLO WORLD

If you haven't done it so far, please create a folder called php in the htdocs folder of your server. Let's start with the hello world example (*Listing 2*).

```
<?php
print('Hello World');
// or
echo 'hello World';
?>
```

Listing 2: hello.php

The PHP interpreter only executes PHP code within its delimiters. Anything outside the delimiters is not processed by PHP. Delimiters are configurable but the most common delimiters are *<?php* to open and *?>* to close PHP sections. If you think of creating PHP codes for a website a more realistic example would be something like listing 3. In this listing you can see the typical mixture of HTML (HTML5) and PHP.

```
<!DOCTYPE html>
<html>
<head>
  <meta http-equiv="Content-Type" content="text/html; charset=UTF-8" />
  <title>Your Website</title>
</head>
<body>
```

```
<header>
  <nav>
    <ul>
      <li>Your menu</li>
    </ul>
  </nav>
</header>

<section>
  <article>
    <header>
    <h2>Article title</h2>
      <p>Posted on <time datetime="<?php echo gmdate("Y-m-d\TH:i:s") ?>"><?
php echo date(DATE_RFC822);?></time> by <a href="#">Author</a></p>
    </header>
    <p>... some text</p>
  </article>
</section>
</body>
</html>
```

Listing 3: hello_html5.php

PHP is not complicated. The biggest problem is to figure out the right syntax and the concepts in general.

VARIABLES

A variable is a symbolic name for a piece of data. The idea behind it is to have a name or a kind of a 'pointer' for this data to be able to use it in a script. The data of the variable may change in one script (*Listing 4*).

```
<?php
$date = date('Y-m-d')
print($date);
// or
echo $date;
?>
```

Listing 4: variable.php

FUNCTIONS

PHP has a lot of inbuilt functions like *print()* or *phpinfo()*. But the real power comes with self made functions that are tailored to your needs. In *listing 5* you see an example of a self made function. In your browser the result will be this sentence **The date is 2011-11-02**.

```
<?php
// this is the function
function writeDate()
```

```
{
  echo date('Y-m-d');
}
// this is the main script
echo "The date is ";
writeDate();
?>
```

Listing 5: function.php

PARAMETERS

It is possible to use parameters in functions and of course in several other places. In the example in *Listing 6*, I use two parameters. The first parameter is the format of the date (*$format*) and the second parameter is the punctuation (*$punctuation*). Parameters can be used as variables in functions.

```
<?php
// this is the function
function writeDate($format, $punctuation)
{
  echo '- <strong>'.$format.'</strong> the display will be ';
  echo '<strong>'.date($format).'</strong>' . $punctuation.'<br />';
}


// this is the main script
echo 'If you write something like: <br/> ';
writedate('Y-m-d',',');
writedate('H:i:s',',');
writedate('m.d.y','.');
writedate('l jS \of F Y h:i:s A','.');
?>
```

Listing 6: parameter.php

In your browser it will look like:

> *If you write something like:*
>
> *- Y-m-d the display will be 2011-11-02,*
>
> *- H:i:s the display will be 18:32:33,*
>
> *- m.d.y the display will be 11.02.11.*
>
> *- l jS \of F Y h:i:s A the display will be Wednesday 2nd of November 2011 06:32:33 PM.*

Return Values

Sometimes you want to outsource some code to a different place, for example a calculation. One possibility is to use a function. The code of the function is always the same but the return value depends on the given parameter.

```php
<?php
function add($x,$y)
{
  $result=$x+$y;
  return $result;
}
echo "13 + 27 = ".add(13,27);
?>
```

CONTROL STRUCTURES

PHP provides the usual suspects:

If Else

If an expression is true like $a >$b execute a statement. If not ... else ... than execute another statement.

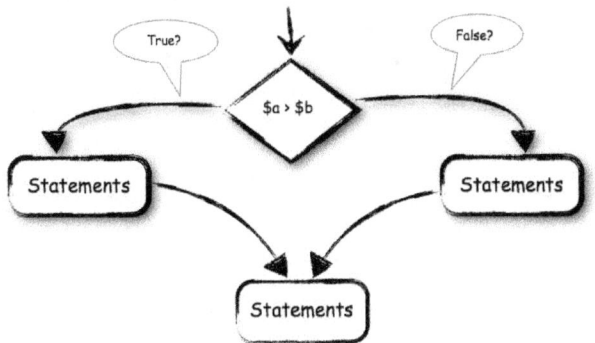

```php
<?php
if ($a > $b) {
  echo "a is greater than b";
} else {
  echo "a is NOT greater than b";
}
?>
```

If Elseif

In this construct it is possible to ask twice if ... elseif ...else.

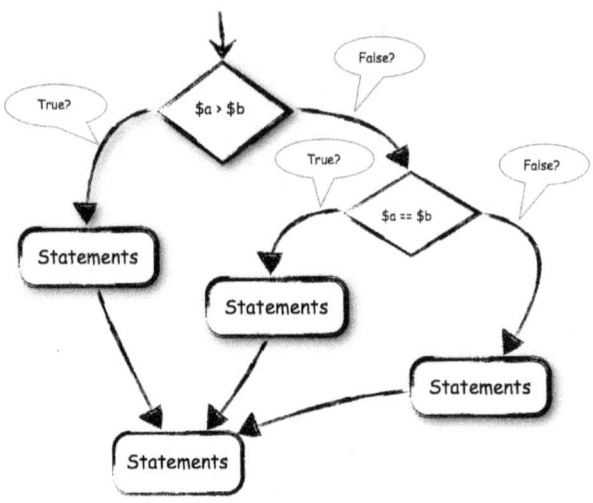

```php
<?php
if ($a > $b) {
    echo "a is bigger than b";
} elseif ($a == $b) {
    echo "a is equal to b";
} else {
    echo "a is smaller than b";
}
?>
```

While

The while loop executes the statement as long as the while expression is TRUE.

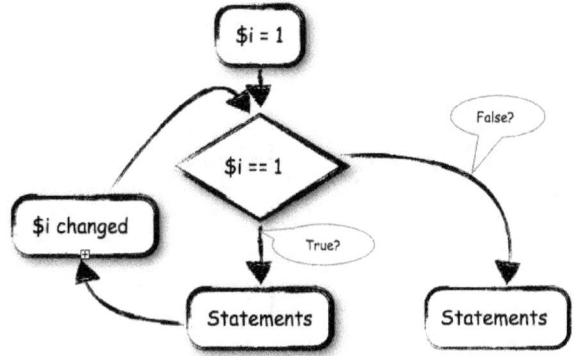

```php
<?php
$i = 1;
while ($i <= 10){
    echo $i;
    $i++;
}
?>
```

Foreach

Foreach iterates over arrays and only works with arrays. An array is a list of values.

```php
<?php
$a = array(1, 2, 3, 17);
foreach ($a as $v) {
    echo "Current value of \$a: $v.\n";
}
?>
```

Switch

The switch statement is similar to a series of if statements on the same expression. If you want to compare the same variable (or expression) with many different values, the switch statement is more elegant than a number of if statements.

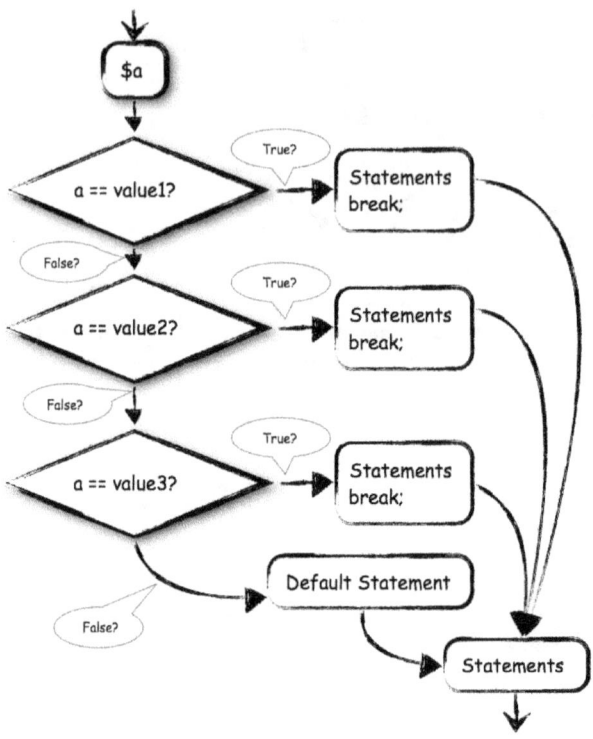

```php
<?php
switch ($i) {
    case 0:
        echo "i equals 0";
        break;
    case 1:
        echo "i equals 1";
        break;
    case 2:
        echo "i equals 2";
        break;
}
```

```
?>
```

CLASSES

The main difference between PHP4 and PHP5 was the rewritten object model. See chapter What is Object Oriented Programming for more information on this topic. A basic example would look like *Listing 7*.

```php
<?php
class Car {
    public $colour;
    public $brand;
    public $image;

    public function __construct($colour, $brand, $image) {
        $this->colour = $colour;
        $this->brand  = $brand;
        $this->image  = $image;
    }

    public function startEngineMethod() {
        return '<img src="'. $this->image .'"> The ' . $this->colour . " " . $this->brand . " starts its engine.";
    }
}

$her_car = new Car('red', 'Ferrari', 'http://farm4.static.flickr.com/
3004/2541945935_422339cbef_t.jpg'); //Photo by exfordy (CC BY 2.0)

$his_car = new Car('blue', 'Smart', 'http://farm1.static.flickr.com/
66/222092351_c9b93d3286_t_d.jpg'); // Photo by cocoate  (CC BY 2.0)

$other_car= new Car('','Volkswagen',    'http://farm4.static.flickr.com/
3040/2746837856_7acb6535c0_t_d.jpg'); // Photo by Glen Edelson  (CC BY 2.0)


echo $her_car->startEngineMethod(); // prints "The red Ferrari starts its
engine."

echo '<hr />';

echo $his_car->startEngineMethod(); // prints "The green Triumph starts its
engine."

echo '<hr />';

echo $other_car->startEngineMethod(); // prints "The Volkswagen starts its
engine."

?>
```

Listing 7: class.php

The result in the browser will look like in *Figure 3*

Figure 3: Output of class.php

By far the best reference for PHP is the documentation on php.net[100]. If you are curious, play around and try out as much as you can[101].

---

[100] http://php.net/

[101] Download the example files on http://cocoate.com/jdev/php

Chapter 19

What Is Object-Oriented Programming?

Object-oriented programming (OOP) is a programming paradigm using "objects" – data structures consisting of data fields and methods together with their interactions – to design applications and computer programs. Programming techniques may include features such as data abstraction, encapsulation, messaging, modularity, polymorphism, and inheritance. Many modern programming languages now support OOP, at least as an option[102].

Translated - the OOP paradigm wants to picture structures and relationships between objects like in the real world!

Some people think it is the best idea on earth since sliced bread, others say, it is the most overrated and overhyped programming paradigm on earth.

As always, the truth is somewhere in the middle.

CLASSES, OBJECTS, INSTANCES, PROPERTIES AND BEHAVIOURS

Before we dive into the dry stuff, let's be clear about the basics of OOP.

---

[102] http://en.wikipedia.org/wiki/Object-oriented_programming

- A class is a concept of an object
- An object is an instance of a class
- An instance has properties (or attributes) and behaviours (or methods) defined by the class

Have a look around where you are sitting at the moment, maybe you see something like *Figure 1*.

Figure 1: Classes and Objects

In OOP a class is a blueprint for an object/instance. In our example the class girl is the general blueprint for all girls and the class boy for all the boys. We have only two classes (blueprints) and all girls and boys (objects) are based on them.

```
class girl {

}

class boy {

}
```

ATTRIBUTES/PROPERTIES

Each girl and each boy have attributes. These attributes are often called properties. The precise meaning of these terms depends often on what language/system/universe we are talking about. In HTML, an attribute is the part of a tag with a kind of a key and a value and property doesn't mean anything, for example. Often, an attribute is used to describe the mechanism or real-world thing. A property is used to describe the model. In the example class we use the properties *$eyecolor* and *$name*.

```
class girl {
  //properties
```

```
   public $eyecolor;
   public $name;
}


class boy {
   //properties
   public $eyecolor;
   public $name;
}
```

When you see the source code you'll notice that our girl and boy classes are quite similar. We know that both are different in many ways but for these examples I don't want to go in deeper details :)

INSTANTIATION

The "birth" of our girl and boy object is called instantiation. The object itself can be called instance too.

```
class girl {
   //properties
   public $eyecolor;
   public $name;
}


class boy {
   //properties
   public $eyecolor;
   public $name;
}
//Instantiation
$harold = new girl('brown', 'Harold Chasen');
$maude = new boy('grey', 'Maude Chardin');
```

The word *new* calls a special method, the constructor method. In this method, all values given by parameters are configured for exactly this instance. These values are unique for each instance.

We created $harold and $maude! Each should have a name and an eye colour. They are kind of "born" :)

METHODS, BEHAVIOURS

Now that we have created two instances, it would be nice to give them a few skills, like the ability to speak, to run, to think ... you name it. These skills are called methods in OOP. Methods define the behaviour of instances. In the code example, a method looks technically like a function. This wording is special to PHP because PHP was not object oriented from the beginning. Luckily, in other languages, a method is usually called method.

```
class girl {
   //properties
```

```
    public $eyecolor;
    public $name;

    //constructor is called while instantiation
    public function __construct($eyecolor, $name) {
        $this->eyecolor = $eyecolor;
        $this->name   = $name;
    }

    //method
    public function sayName() {
        return 'My name is '. $this->name;
    }
}

class boy {
    //properties
    public $eyecolor;
    public $name;

    //constructor is called while instantiation
    public function __construct($eyecolor, $name) {
        $this->eyecolor = $eyecolor;
        $this->name   = $name;
    }

    //method
    public function sayName() {
        return 'My name ist '. $this->name;
    }
}


//Instantiation
$harold = new girl('brown', 'Harold Chasen');
$maude = new boy('grey', 'Maude Chardin');
```

ACCESS RIGHTS

In front of the word *function* you see the word *public*. *Public* is an access right. Even if our instances are virtual, they need public and private areas. A public method can be called from "outside" of the class, a private method only from "inside" of the class. In our example, the method *sayName* is public. That means, someone can call *$harold->sayName()* and Harold will do so. The reality of human beings is a bit more complicated. Harold would have to learn a language first and then he would need a "decision" method (or a brain method), whether he wants to answer or not. Harold's method of speaking would be a private one in reality, called by the "decision" method because only Harold or to be more precise Harold's "decision" method should decide whether he wants to speak or not.

```
//Instantiation
$harold = new boy('brown', 'Harold Chasen');
```

```
//Method call
$harold->sayName()
```

The result of this little script would be *"My name is Harold Chasen"*.

HOW TO USE THE OOP PARADIGM IN A WEBSITE?

In our example, we have one or more classes. These classes could be stored in one file or in separate files. It's up to you. Let's say, we create a file girl.php and a file boy.php with the inherent method. These classes have no user interface. The methods will be called by another script.

If someone is visiting your website he may decide to create a user account. He fills in a form and clicks on the register button. Values like the name will be transferred to the method and this is the time where the instantiation will occur. Harold and Maude could be users of our websites afterwards.

Chapter 20

What Is MooTools?

a compact javascript framework

MooTools is a compact, modular, Object-Oriented JavaScript framework designed for the intermediate to advanced JavaScript developer. It allows you to write powerful, flexible, and cross-browser code with its elegant, well documented, and coherent API.

MooTools code respects strict standards and doesn't throw any warnings. It's extensively documented and has meaningful variable names: a joy to browse and a snap to understand.

Open Source License

MooTools is released under the Open Source MIT license, which gives you the possibility to use it and modify it in every circumstance.

Browser Compatibility

MooTools is compatible and fully tested with Safari, Internet Explorer 6+, Firefox, Opera, and Chrome.

http://mootools.net/

MooTools is a JavaScript Framework. The name MooTools is derived from *My Object-Oriented Tools* and that the object orientation is probably one reason why the Joomla! project leaders decided to use MooTools as the inbuilt default JavaScript Framework in Joomla!.

Compared to native JavaScript, a framework like MooTools has significant advantages.

- It follows object-oriented practices and the *"Don't repeat yourself"* (DRY) principle. It offers amazing effects and enhancements to the *Document Object Model (DOM)*, enabling developers to easily add, modify, select, and delete DOM elements.

- It supports storing and retrieving information with element storage.

- It offers built-in functions for manipulation of CSS, native JavaScript objects and Ajax requests.

- It provides an *Application Programming Interface (API)* as well as a custom downloads module allowing developers to download and use only the modules and dependencies they need for a particular app.

If you do not fully understand all of the advantages, don't be scared. One other advantage of the combination Joomla! and MooTools is, that it is not necessary to know JavaScript in all its facets to use a great part of the MooTools magic. You learn and understand more and more JavaScript by using the MooTools functions regularly.

WHY MOOTOOLS?

To face one of the biggest questions at the beginning of this chapter, I want to talk shortly about jQuery - the "other" JavaScript Framework.

Because of the fact that MooTools is already inbuilt in the Joomla! CMS you are not facing the challenging task of picking the right framework to use. A few years ago there were many JavaScript frameworks on the market and they were widely used. Since the decision of Microsoft to use and support jQuery as "their" JavaScript Framework for Visual Studio and other projects in the year 2008 each other JavaScript framework has to explain why it exists :) In the case of MooTools, there is a very clear and honest website in different languages available dedicated to the topic jQuery vs MooTools[103]. If you really need jQuery in Joomla!, it is possible and other developers do so (jQuery++ Integrator[104]).

DEMOS

It is interesting to read what's possible but it's always better to see the possibilities live in a web browser. For this purpose the MooTools team provides a demo site[105].

You can explore demonstrations from different parts of the framework. In Figure 1 you see the Drag and Drop example in an e-commerce use case. It is possible to drag t-shirts into a cart.

Figure 1: Drag and Drop example on MooTools.net

All the examples are based on MooTools without the Joomla! CMS. You can see the source code in an online editor.

JOOMLA! AND MOOTOOLS

Joomla! uses MooTools in many places and usually you do not have to write JavaScript Code to use it in your extensions.

It starts with the installer. Maybe you already noticed the little wheel that appears when you install Joomla! go from step to step. It's made with the help of MooTools (Figure 2).

---

[103] http://jqueryvsmootools.com/

[104] http://extensions.joomla.org/extensions/core-enhancements/scripts/12995

[105] http://mootools.net/demos

Figure 2: MooTools in the Joomla! Installer

Other examples in Joomla! are the slider and the tabs in the default beez_20 Template located on position-4, and position-8 (Figure 3, Figure 4).

Figure 3: MooTools in Beez Slider

Figure 4: MooTools in Beez Tabs

You find more examples by strolling through the Joomla! administration interface.

A TOOLTIP EXAMPLE

To make life easier for developers who want to use the basic MooTools effects, the JavaScript Code is encapsulated in Joomla classes. You do not need any know-how of JavaScript to use them.

Let's have a look at the tooltips. I am sure you have noticed the Joomla! tooltips in the backend (*Figure 5*).

Figure 5: Tooltips in Joomla! backend

First I want to have a tooltip when hovering over the sponsoring link of the example module (*mod_coco_bookfeed*[106]). To integrate a tooltip I only need one additional line of code on top of the template file *default.php*.

```
JHTML::_('behavior.tooltip');
```

JHTML is a class with a static method that creates the tooltip. If you are curious, you can find the source code of the behaviour class and long comments in */libraries/joomla/html/html/ behaviour.php* as part of the Joomla! platform. The method is looking for a the HTML attribute class with the value hasTip. So as second step we have to add this attribute class="hasTip" in the desired link.

```
<a class="hasTip"
   title="YOURTITLE::YOURTITLE"
   href="http://cocoate.com/sponsoring"
   target="_blank">
   YOURLINKDESCRIPTION</a>
```

If it finds the class it will append the tooltip like in Figure 6. It simply work without any knowledge of MooTools.

---

[106] https://github.com/hagengraf/mod_coco_bookfeed

Figure 6: Tooltips in example module

It's also possible to connect tooltips to text with the span attribute.

```
<span class="hasTip"
    title="YOURTITLE::YOURTITLE">
    Hover on this text to see the tooltip</span>
```

CUSTOMISED TOOLTIPS WITH CSS

If you want to customise the design of the default tooltip, you have to insert CSS code. Let's enhance our tooltip.

You should store the CSS statements in an external file and put them in a folder /css in your extension (*Listing 1*).

```
/* Tooltips */
.tip-wrap {
    float: left;
    border: 5px solid #417FCC;
    max-width: 200px;
    border-radius: 5px;
-moz-border-radius: 5px;
-webkit-border-radius: 5px;
}
.tip-title {
    padding: 3px;
    margin: 0;
    background: #fff;
    font-size: 120%;
    font-weight: bold;
```

```
}
.tip-text {
    font-size: 110%;
    padding:3px;
    background: #fff;
    border-radius: 5px;
-moz-border-radius: 5px;
-webkit-border-radius: 5px;
}
```

Listing 1: /modules/mod_coco_bookfeed/css/mod_coco_bookfeed.css

You can load the file in the view of your extension (mostly named *default.php*) with the following code

```
// Add a reference to a CSS file
// The default path is 'media/system/css/'
$css_filename = 'mod_coco_bookfeed.css';
$css_path = 'modules/mod_coco_bookfeed/css/';
JHTML::stylesheet($css_filename, $css_path);
```

Tooltips Structure

To be able to write the correct CSS statements you need the structure of the tooltips in Joomla! 1.7

```
<div class="tip-wrap">
    <div class="tip-top"></div>
    <div class="tip">
        <div class="tip-title"></div>
        <div class="tip-text"></div>
    </div>
    <div class="tip-bottom"></div>
</div>
```

The result will look different like in *Figure 7*.

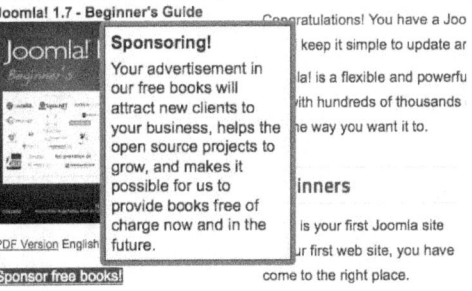

Figure 7: Customised Tooltip

MULTIPLE CUSTOMISED TOOLTIPS

If you want to have different styled tooltips you need an additional class as a trigger for JHTML and of course different CSS statements.

Let's say your customised tooltips should appear when a class called hasCustomTip is used in an HTML tag (remember the trigger for the default tooltips is hasTip). To manage the different CSS classes you have to add a third parameter to the JHTML class. Here are the two lines you need.

```
$toolTipArray = array('className'=>'custom');

JHTML::_('behavior.tooltip', '.hasCustomTip', $toolTipArray);
```

In your CSS file you need the additional custom classes.

```
/* Custom Tooltips */
.custom .tip-wrap {
    float: left;
    border: 5px solid #417FCC;
    max-width: 200px;
    border-radius: 5px;
     -moz-border-radius: 5px;
     -webkit-border-radius: 5px;
}


.custom .tip-title {
    padding: 3px;
    margin: 0;
    background: red;
    font-size: 120%;
    font-weight: bold;
}


.custom .tip-text {
    font-size: 110%;
    padding:3px;
    background: #fff;
    border-radius: 5px;
     -moz-border-radius: 5px;
     -webkit-border-radius: 5px;
}
```

The default HTML looks like this

```
<span
  class="hasTip"
  title="hasTip Title::This is using the default class 'hasTip'.">
```

```
hasTip hover text</span>
```

The customised HTML uses the other trigger class.

```
<span
  class="hasCustomTip"
    title="hasCustomTip Title::This is using the customised class
'hasCustomTip'.">
  hasCustomTip hover text</span>
```

You can configure as many different styles as you need.

RESOURCES

This was just a short example to introduce MooTools. See also

- http://mootorial.com/

- http://api.joomla.org/Joomla-Platform/HTML/JHtml.html

www.cocoate.com

cocoate.com

is the publisher of this book and an independent management consultancy, based in France and working internationally.
Specialised in three areas – Consulting, Coaching and Teaching – cocoate.com develops web based strategies for process and project management and public relations; provides customised trainings for open source content management systems Drupal, Joomla! and WordPress, in the area of management and leadership skills and develops educational projects with the focus on non-formal learning.

The European educational projects focus on the promotion of lifelong learning with the goal of social integration. Particular emphasis is placed on learning methods in order to learn how to learn, the conception and realisation of cross-generational learning strategies and local community development.

http://cocoate.com